TWENTIETH CENTURY
INTERPRETATIONS

MAYNARD MACK, *Series Editor*
Yale University

NOW AVAILABLE
Collections of Critical Essays
ON

ADVENTURES OF HUCKLEBERRY FINN
ALL FOR LOVE
ARROWSMITH
AS YOU LIKE IT
THE BOOK OF JOB
THE DUCHESS OF MALFI
THE FROGS
SIR GAWAIN AND THE GREEN KNIGHT
THE GREAT GATSBY
GULLIVER'S TRAVELS
HAMLET
HENRY IV, PART TWO
HENRY V
THE ICEMAN COMETH
THE PORTRAIT OF A LADY
SAMSON AGONISTES
THE SCARLET LETTER
THE SOUND AND THE FURY
TOM JONES
TWELFTH NIGHT
UTOPIA
WALDEN
THE WASTE LAND

TWENTIETH CENTURY INTERPRETATIONS
OF

TOM JONES

TWENTIETH CENTURY INTERPRETATIONS
OF
TOM JONES

A Collection of Critical Essays

Edited by
MARTIN C. BATTESTIN

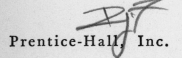

Prentice-Hall, Inc. *Englewood Cliffs, N. J.*

A SPECTRUM BOOK

Current printing (last number):
10 9 8 7 6 5 4 3 2 1

Contents

Introduction

by Martin C. Battestin

I

Tom Jones (1749) is at once the last and the consummate literary achievement of England's Augustan age. Notwithstanding the whimsy of Dr. Leavis, who finds life too short for the reading of very many masterpieces, the place Henry Fielding's finest novel holds in "the great tradition" of English fiction is quite secure. Not just as the mirror of the manners and ethos of an age or as the germinative influence behind such different writers as Jane Austen and Dickens, Thackeray and George Eliot, Saul Bellow and John Barth but as a work of art in its own right, *Tom Jones* recently has been the subject of more stimulating critical discussion than any other novel of its period.

To be sure, in our century as in his own, Fielding has suffered from the criticisms of those who either have misunderstood his fiction or have found it not very much to their taste. The grounds of Dr. Johnson's preference for Samuel Richardson, "who knew how a watch was made," over Fielding, who could merely "tell the hour by looking on the dial-plate," are not very far from those of Ian Watt's, who distinguishes, to Fielding's disadvantage, between Richardson's technique of "formal realism" and Fielding's "realism of assessment." Between them these two great novelists, in conscious rivalry, marked out the divergent directions that modern fiction was to take—Richardson in *Pamela* (1740) and *Clarissa* (1747–48) turning inward to explore the dark corners of the personality, Fielding in *Joseph Andrews* (1742) and *Tom Jones* ranging outward to encompass the variegated panorama of society. In their best and most representative works, *Clarissa* and *Tom Jones,* the differences that separate these authors are absolute, as diametrical as the difference between tragedy and comedy, between the novel of character and the novel of manners and action, between the "realistic" mode and the paradigmatic.

Inevitably, therefore, the claims of Richardson and of Fielding for pre-eminence have been debated by readers for more than two centuries. In his own day, the most damaging charge against Fielding was the "lowness" of his themes—his preoccupation with the adventures (chiefly sexual) of footmen and foundlings, of country wenches and Mayfair demi-reps. Dr. Johnson was appalled that Hannah More had read so "vicious," so "corrupt" a book as *Tom Jones,* and a writer in *Old England* fancied that the earthquakes that shook London in 1750 were signs of God's wrath at the enthusiastic reception accorded Fielding's novel. But the very qualities that offended the prudish and the proper among Fielding's first readers have recommended *Tom Jones* to a twentieth-century audience; Fielding's wit and hearty good humor and, above all, his tolerant humanity have seemed more congenial to us than has the sober—one might almost say pathological—prudentialism of Richardson, however compelling the force of his art in a book like *Clarissa.*

We are, in fact, still very much in the midst of the "Fielding revival" that Kingsley Amis remarked ten years ago, one sign of which has been the brilliant success of the recent film *Tom Jones.* In *The New York Times Book Review* for July 7, 1957, Amis observed that Fielding's humor was "closer to our own than that of any writer before the present century," and he further found that in rejecting "the novel of consistent tone," contemporary authors have followed Fielding in attempting "to combine the violent and the absurd, the grotesque and the romantic, the farcical and the horrific within a single novel." One thinks, for example, of Saul Bellow's *Adventures of Augie March,* of John Barth's *The Sot-Weed Factor,* and of Amis's own *Lucky Jim* as books in which Fielding would have recognized a form and an impulse similar to his own. The fact of Fielding's relevance to the novelists of our new Age of Satire is perhaps most eloquently stated by Bowen, the young writer of Amis's *I Like It Here,* who, standing before the white stone sarcophagus in which the author of *Tom Jones* rests near Lisbon, reflects upon the significance of the master:

> Bowen thought about Fielding. Perhaps it was worth dying in your forties if two hundred years later you were the only noncontemporary novelist who could be read with unaffected and wholehearted interest, the only one who never had to be apologized for or excused on the grounds of changing taste. And how enviable to live in the world of his novels, where duty was plain, evil arose out of malevolence and a starving wayfarer could be invited indoors without hesitation and without fear. Did that make it a simplified world? Perhaps, but that hardly mattered beside the existence of a moral seriousness that could be made apparent without the aid of evangelical puffing and blowing.[1]

Other reasons for the reputation *Tom Jones* now enjoys are given by the critics who are brought together in the present anthology. Empson, for example, stresses Fielding's moral perceptiveness, and Wright his

---

[1] From Kingsley Amis, *I Like It Here* (New York: Harcourt, Brace & World, Inc., 1958), p. 185. Quoted by permission of the publishers, Harcourt, Brace and World, Inc., and Curtis Brown, Ltd. (London).

delight in artifice and what might be called (to alter a phrase from Matthew Arnold) his high playfulness. Professor Crane, an Aristotelian of a somewhat different stamp from Fielding himself, discloses the intricate architecture of the novel's famous plot, while Booth examines the function of the intrusive narrator, and Alter considers the various devices and effects of Fielding's style. The variety of the approaches represented in these essays testifies to the complexity and richness of *Tom Jones*.

II

As Booth has observed, the most important "character" in *Tom Jones* is the narrator himself, whose voice, as he relates the story to his "good-natured" and hopefully "sagacious" reader or as he digresses in his comments and prefaces, sounds very like Fielding's own. More than any other major novelist of the period, Henry Fielding—or rather that heightened and idealized projection of him which has been called his "second-self"—is immanent in his book. From the first sentence to the last, he is, to use his own analogy (XVIII.i), the reader's close companion on this stagecoach journey through the imaginary world of the novel. It is useful, therefore, to know something about the man whose wit entertains us and whose genial wisdom instructs.

The circumstances of Fielding's life and, what is more important, the force of his convictions—political, religious, and critical—in large part determined the particular shape and character of *Tom Jones*. Though this is neither an autobiographical novel nor a *roman à clef*, Fielding's constant method as a writer of fiction was to translate the particular facts of his experience into symbols of universal relevance. Consider, for instance, the setting of the book. Paradise Hall, where Fielding's foundling hero was born and raised, is, like Eden itself, an imaginary estate. Yet it is composed of elements associated in the novelist's mind with his own heritage, his own ideal identity: the distinctive features of Allworthy's seat are drawn both from the estates of Fielding's benefactors, George Lyttelton and Ralph Allen, and more especially from the prospect westward from atop Tor Hill in Glastonbury, Somerset, which, though Fielding does not mention it by name, may be taken as the specific locale of the novel's first six books. From the threshold at Sharpham Park, the home of Fielding's maternal grandfather and the place of the novelist's birth in 1707, Glastonbury Tor rises in full view only a short distance across the moors. The roads Tom Jones follows from Glastonbury to Wells, Gloucester, Upton-upon-Severn, and Meriden and at last from Coventry to London are those Fielding often had traveled, and the time of Tom's journey is that critical moment in the late autumn of 1745 when the Jacobite rebels under the Young Pretender, Charles Edward Stuart, had crossed the Tweed and were advancing deep into the heart of England.

Certain of the principal characters in the novel, furthermore, were broadly modeled on Fielding's friends and acquaintances. Lyttelton and Allen are reflected in Squire Allworthy, and Sophia Western, the girl whom Tom Jones loves and marries, is in part an idealization of Fielding's first wife, Charlotte Cradock—"one," he declared before her death in 1744, "from whom I draw all the solid comfort of my life." To notice these correspondences is by no means to imply that *Tom Jones* is not a work of fiction after all, but a mere transcription of actuality. Fielding's true subect, announced in the first chapter, is "HUMAN NATURE"; the world he presents is an imaginative creation, more symbol than fact, and his hero's progress is ultimately the journey, at least as arduous as amusing, we all must take from innocence to wisdom. In *Joseph Andrews* (III.i) Fielding declared, "once for all, I describe not men, but manners; not an individual, but a species"; yet he added, "I believe I might aver that I have writ little more than I have seen." Although *Tom Jones* is finally concerned with universals—with presenting, as Fielding said of *Don Quixote,* "the history of the world in general"—it is also a book, like Joyce's *Ulysses,* firmly rooted in the soil of contemporary life.

More important than the actual people and events reflected in the novel are the factors in Fielding's experience that helped to condition his attitudes and thought. Both by birth and by education, Fielding was a gentleman, proud of his family's connection with the aristocracy and intellectually at home in the great Christian humanist tradition. His father, though too improvident to leave him much money, was a military man who rose to the rank of General; his mother, Sarah Gould, was the daughter of a judge. After a childhood spent in the country village of East Stour, Dorset—a fact perhaps reflected in the novels, in which the naturalness and simplicity of the country provide the antithesis to the affectation and vice of the town—Fielding received an excellent formal education, first at Eton College (1719–24) and then at the University of Leyden (1728–29), across the Channel in Holland. From this period stems the intimate knowledge of the classics and of their ancient and modern commentators that informs nearly everything he wrote and that lies behind his conception of the novel itself, the "new species of writing" he introduced into English literature and called the "comic epic-poem in prose."

In need of money, as he always seems to have been, Fielding returned from Holland determined to make his mark as a dramatist in London. From 1730 to 1737, he produced more than a score of plays—all of them comedies, farces, or satires. Most popular were *Tom Thumb* (1730), an hilarious burlesque of heroic tragedy, and *Pasquin* (1736) and *The Historical Register* (1737), political satires aimed chiefly, and to Fielding's cost, at the Prime Minister, Sir Robert Walpole. As Colley Cibber remarked in a passage in his autobiography typical of the wit for which he is celebrated in Pope's *Dunciad*, Fielding, "like another Erostratus, set fire to his stage, by writing up to an Act of Parliament to demolish it": Fielding's satires so incensed the Minister that he forced the passage of the Licensing Act of 1737, which closed the doors of Fielding's Little Theatre in the Haymarket and ended his career as a playwright. If Fielding was the most successful dramatist of his time, whose plays may still be read with enjoyment, it is surely too much to say, with Bernard Shaw, that he was "the greatest dramatist, with the single exception of Shakespear, produced by England between the Middle Ages and the nineteenth century." [2] His years as a playwright were important primarily for what they meant to the novels: the theater sharpened Fielding's ear for comic dialogue and perfected that sense of form, of significant design, which is one of his chief contributions to the art of fiction.

Although the period between the end of Fielding's theatrical career and the publication of *Tom Jones* was too eventful to be traced here in detail, yet it is too important to an understanding of that novel to be ignored. Having married in 1734, Fielding found himself three years later with no apparent means of supporting his family. In November, 1737, he entered the Middle Temple, determined to prepare himself for the law. Less than three years later, he was called to the Bar, but despite his diligence in term time and on the Western Circuit, he could not make a living at his new profession. To supplement his meager income, he was obliged to turn hackney author; it was preferable, he once facetiously remarked, to becoming a hackney coachman. During 1739–41, he renewed his attacks against the man who had driven him from the stage, editing *The Champion* and publishing a number of pamphlets and poems calculated to serve the Opposition's cause against Walpole. But the great event of this period was literary rather than political—the appearance in November, 1740, of Richardson's first novel, *Pamela: or, Virtue Rewarded*. At once exasperated and amused at the enthusiastic reception accorded the epistolary adventures of Richardson's shrewdly chaste young servant maid, Fielding responded first by parodying the book in *Shamela* (1741) and then by offering in *Joseph Andrews* (1742) his own alternative conception of the art of the novel. Though less ambitious, and perhaps less profound, than *Tom Jones*, *Joseph Andrews* is none the less the first masterful comic novel in English. In the theory set forth in his preface and introductory chap-

---

[2] Shaw's *Plays: Pleasant and Unpleasant* (New York: Brentano's, 1909), I, xiii.

ters, and in the deft execution of the narrative, Fielding had invented a new genre, which he called the "comic romance" or "comic epic-poem in prose"—a new literary form whose promise and potential he fully realized in *Tom Jones*. For our present purpose, only one other production of this period need be mentioned, the collection in three volumes of Fielding's *Miscellanies* (1743). Except for *Jonathan Wild*, the pieces here assembled are undistinguished in themselves, but valuable for the light they shed on the novels. In verse epistles such as "Of Good-Nature" and "Of True Greatness," or in essays such as "On Conversation" and "On the Knowledge of the Characters of Men," Fielding sets forth discursively the values and ethical beliefs that are enacted dramatically in the characters of Parson Adams and Tom Jones, of Allworthy and Dr. Harrison, of Jonathan Wild and Blifil.

In July, 1744, Fielding contributed to the second edition of his sister's novel *The Adventures of David Simple* a preface in which he affected to despise the insubstantial favors of the Muse, protesting that he had neither leisure nor inclination to write another work of fiction. This resolution happily was short-lived, for to judge from internal evidence, he was soon—perhaps even before the year was out—to begin work on his masterpiece. From the fact that the first six books of *Tom Jones* contain not a single definite allusion to the Jacobite uprising (and from certain other evidence too complex to be presented here), it seems clear that Fielding had finished about a third of the novel before the late summer of 1745, when news of the rebellion interrupted him. By October of that year and for several months thereafter, there were matters more urgent than novel-writing to occupy him. In earnest support of the Hanoverian Establishment, he published in rapid succession three hortatory pamphlets designed to acquaint the public with the pernicious consequences of a Jacobite victory and to arouse them in defense of their Constitution and religion. These works, issued within a fortnight in October, 1745, were *A Serious Address to the People of Great Britain, The History of the Present Rebellion,* and *A Dialogue between the Devil, the Pope, and the Pretender*. The same motives prompted him to undertake *The True Patriot,* a weekly journal that he conducted from November 5, 1745, to June 17, 1746. The winter of 1745 was indeed bleak and ominous—a critical moment in England's history, when the political and religious institutions Fielding cherished were threatened by a successful rebellion at home and when the war with France was going badly on the Continent. These dark and perilous months chilled his spirits and continued to trouble his thoughts long after the immediate danger had passed. It was a time, he recalled, when the nation was faltering at "the very Brink of Ruin" (*True Patriot*, April 22–29, 1746), a time "far more terrible to all the Lovers of Liberty and the Protestant

Religion, than this Age had ever seen before, or is, I hope, in any Danger of seeing again" (*Jacobite's Journal*, August 13, 1748). No wonder, then, that when he returned to *Tom Jones* after the Jacobites had been defeated at Culloden (April 16, 1746), Fielding set the action of his central narrative in November, 1745, "the very time when the late rebellion was at the highest" (VII.xi), or that he made his hero—"a hearty well-wisher to the glorious cause of liberty, and of the Protestant religion"— volunteer to join the King's forces marching north against the rebels.

Since the fall of Walpole in 1742 and the formation of the so-called "Broad-Bottom" Administration in 1744, the government now included many of the men whom Fielding most admired—among them Lyttelton and the Duke of Bedford, to name the two he compliments in the dedication to *Tom Jones*. The "Forty-five" having drawn him back into politics, this time on the side of the ministry, Fielding continued to support his friends in print, most notably in *The Jacobite's Journal* (December 5, 1747–November 5, 1748), the irony of whose title points at the Tory Opposition, that ardent and vociferous faction whose principles Fielding was at the same time writing into the memorable character of Squire Western. For his services to the government, Fielding was rewarded, shortly before the publication of *Tom Jones*, by being appointed Justice of the Peace, first for the City of Westminster and then also for the County of Middlesex. Though the Opposition journalists sneered, Fielding brought to his new office an energetic concern for the cause of justice and the public welfare that few of his predecessors could boast of. As satirist and now as magistrate, he constantly addressed himself to the betterment of society, to the detection of vice and the correction of folly. In the few remaining years of his life, he worked to reform the bench and to control the spreading evils of crime and poverty, devoting himself so assiduously to these tasks that he injured his health. By refusing the lucrative perquisites by which his predecessors had made a "job" of the administration of justice, he also suffered financially. These years, moreover, appear to have exacted their price spiritually. In his last novel, *Amelia* (1751), as in his other writings of the fifties (*The Covent-Garden Journal* and the pamphlets on crime and the poor), the genial, easy voice of the narrator of *Tom Jones* has changed to tones graver and more constrained. Fielding's wit and eloquence remain, but the feast of life he celebrated in *Tom Jones* has staled for him. Whatever the cause, whether the sobering effects of his magistracy or the pain he suffered from the hideous disease that killed him, no one who reads that last sad testament of his life, *The Journal of a Voyage to Lisbon* (1755), can fail to be moved by Fielding's weariness and disenchantment. He died in Lisbon on October 8, 1754.

III

Although, as we have said, Fielding is immanent in *Tom Jones,* it is the novel itself, his "great creation" (X.i), that is the subject of the present volume. Despite the petulant protests by Richardson and by Dr. Johnson, *Tom Jones* was a splendid and instantaneous success. Tirelessly "puffed" by Fielding's friends Lyttelton and William Pitt, who had read the work in manuscript, the entire first edition of 2,000 copies was sold before the announced date of publication, February 10, 1749. It was, as Joseph Spence observed with admiration, "perhaps an unheard-of case." By the end of that month, a second edition, of 1,500 copies, was issued, and before the year was out, two further editions had been called for, together amounting to 6,500 copies. Richardson persisted in his haughty refusal to read the book, but clearly he set no very influential example. *Tom Jones,* as even Fielding's antagonists had to admit, was "in every Hand, from the beardless Youth, up to the hoary Hairs of Age." The fact of its popularity did not, to be sure, discourage Fielding's critics from roundly damning a book "so truly profligate, of such evil Tendency, and offensive to every chaste Reader, so discouraging to Virtue and detrimental to Religion!" Such was the opinion expressed by "Aretine" in *Old England* (May 27, 1749) and echoed at length by "Orbilius," his colleague in pseudonymous invective, in the *Examen* of the novel published in December. Yet there were other, juster voices to praise it. Fresh from reading Fielding's "Amazing entertainment," Captain Lewis Thomas exclaimed in a letter to a friend on April 3, 1749: "Character, Painting, Reflexions, Humour, excellent each in its Kind. . . . If my design had been to propagate virtue by appearing publickly in its defence, I should rather have been ye Author of Tom Jones than of five Folio Volumes of sermons."

Indeed, as Fielding declared in dedicating his book to Lyttelton, to recommend "the cause of religion and virtue" had been his "sincere endeavour" in writing *Tom Jones.* To understand how he achieved that purpose in a work of art is to know what Fielding understood by "religion" and "virtue," and what he conceived to be the art of the novel. Though Fielding, like Tom Jones, was a hearty well-wisher to the Protestant religion, his membership in the Church of England was of a very different sort from that of Thwackum, the ferocious and pharisaical upholder of orthodoxy who demonstrates the doctrines of natural depravity and grace by frequent applications of birch to the posteriors of his pupils. "When I mention religion," Thwackum declares, "I mean the Christian religion; and not only the Christian religion, but the Protestant religion; and not only the Protestant religion, but the Church of England" (III.iii). Unlike Thwackum, his author was a Christian of the Low-Church, Latitudinarian tradition, whose chief spokesman in the eighteenth century, the controversial Bishop Benjamin Hoadly, Fielding compliments early in the novel (II.vii). As set forth by Hoadly —and earlier by Isaac Barrow and John Tillotson, whom Fielding also admired and drew upon in his works—the Latitudinarian position was essentially rationalist and mystery-dispelling. In striving for greater comprehension within the Church, and in attempting to accommodate Christianity to an Age of Reason, Hoadly preached that the Church of Christ was nothing less than the whole community of believers. He argued that the Sacrament of the Lord's Supper had no special efficacy, but was instituted merely as a memorial of Christ's sacrifice and as an occasion for renewing Christian feelings of brotherhood. Stressing the importance of works over faith, the Latitudinarians in effect revived the old quarrel between Pelagius and Augustine: man, they maintained against Hobbes and Calvin, was by nature capable of much goodness, and he was free to choose between virtue and vice. As George Whitefield plainly saw (he was the fiery evangelist who, together with Wesley, had begun the Methodist movement in the 1730's), the tendency of such principles was to de-emphasize the role of Christ in salvation and to transform Christianity into a moral system hardly distinguishable from the Stoicism of Cicero or the Deism of Shaftesbury. To Fielding, the religion of Whitefield and his followers, as Parson Adams declares in *Joseph Andrews* (I.xvii), was at best mere "nonsense and enthusiasm," at worst a "pernicious" and "detestable" doctrine; for a persuasion that salvation was a matter of belief rather than virtuous practice, of the passive receiving of grace rather than an active charity, could lead only to the subversion of society. For Fielding, Whitefield, more than any other Englishman of his time, was the Enemy, his doctrine a convenient rationale for the selfish and hypocritical. In *Tom Jones,* the despicable Captain Blifil is "not a little suspected of an inclination to Methodism" (I.x), and his son, the villain of the piece, is last heard of as a member of "that sect" (XVIII.xiii). When Tom Jones pauses to refresh himself at an inn owned by Whitefield's brother (VIII.viii), the evangelist himself, together with his "pernicious principles," becomes the subject of a sardonic digression.

Fielding's morality and his religion are founded upon the benevolist theories inculcated by the Latitudinarians and given additional currency by Shaftesbury. "Good nature," that innate sympathetic disposition which causes us to feel the happiness and misfortunes of others and prompts us to do whatever we can to promote the one and relieve the other, is the chief virtue in his system. The "glorious lust of doing good," he called it in his verse essay on the subject. In order to be meaningful, however, the generous impulses of the good-natured man must be expressed in practice. So it is that Allworthy, like his author, represents an active charity as "an indispensable duty, enjoined both by the Christian law, and by the law of nature itself" (II.v). All the good men of Fielding's fiction share this conviction. He did not believe, of course, that everyone was capable of that high pitch of benevolence evident in a Parson Adams or a Tom Jones. With Pope, Fielding subscribed to the theory of a predominant passion that in part accounted for the individual characters of different men; self-love was as powerful as social, and more generally to be met with. For every Tom Jones, he implies, there is a Blifil. Nevertheless, assisted by the compelling incentives of religion, men could, through the proper exercise of reason and the will, live virtuously and charitably, thereby contributing to the health of society and of the private soul. In all this, Fielding preferred the practical Christianity of the Latitudinarians to the insubstantial theories of deists such as his own philosopher Square, whose abstract speculations on "the natural beauty of virtue" and "the eternal fitness of things" prove inadequate to the business of life. Square's deism, a mixture of vague notions drawn from Shaftesbury and from the intellectualist school of Tindal, flatters the philosopher's opinion of himself but provides no effective moral imperative. His exposure in Molly Seagrim's bedroom (V.v)—a scene which, as the hilarious revelation of the naked truth behind the drapery of pretension, may be taken as the quintessential dramatization of Fielding's theory of "the true Ridiculous"—demonstrates the irrelevancy of Square's metaphysics to the moral life. At the end of the novel (XVIII.iv) his conversion makes the point explicit.

IV

The ideals of good nature and charity, and the tenets of Latitudinarian Christianity, may be said to define, in a general way, the ethos of all Fielding's fiction. Yet Fielding gave to each of his novels a distinctive character and theme of its own: the mock heroics of *Joseph Andrews* define the nature of Chastity and Charity; the irony of *Jonathan Wild* explores the meaning of Greatness; *Amelia* is the rather sentimental story of a marriage. To grasp the distinctive character and purpose of Fielding's masterpiece, we should return to the assertion this essay begins with, that *Tom Jones* represents the consummate literary achievement of England's Augustan age. There are many ways of defining Augustanism, all of them perhaps equally true and all equally in need of qualification. For the present, mine centers upon the correlative ideas of Art and Order that distinguish much of the thought of the age of Newton and Pope— an age whose cast of mind saw the moral drama of the individual life enacted within a frame of cosmic and social order conceived in the then still compatible terms of Christian humanism and Newtonian science, and whose view of art, conditioned by the principles of neo-

Aristotelian aesthetics, saw the poem as fundamentally mimetic of this universal design. The philosophic and aesthetic assumptions of the Augustan age are perhaps most memorably and explicitly expressed in Pope's complementary poems, the *Essay on Criticism* (1711) and the *Essay on Man* (1733–34), in which the neoclassical concept of Nature and of the poetic imitation of her are set forth in couplets as finely wrought and balanced as the poet's universe itself. The point is most succinctly made in these familiar lines from the poem that, Fielding once remarked, *"taught me a System of Philosophy in* English *Numbers"*:

> All Nature is but Art, unknown to thee;
> All Chance, Direction, which thou canst not see;
> All Discord, Harmony, not understood;
> All partial Evil, universal Good. . . .

Pope's universe is Fielding's; Art and Order are its distinguishing characteristics, as they should be of the poem or novel that seeks to imitate "what really exists" (to cite Fielding's translation of Aristotle in *Tom Jones*, VII.i), and as they will be of the microcosm, man, as long as he realizes his true identity. More than any other production of the age— more even than the *Essay on Man*, which presents a similar doctrine in discursive form—*Tom Jones* embodies this philosophy in a work of the creative imagination.

Art, in this peculiarly Augustan sense, is both the subject and the characteristic of *Tom Jones*. To promote "the cause of religion and virtue," as Fielding promised in his dedication, the major themes of the novel are the assertion of the doctrine of Providence, or "the Art of God," and the recommendation of Prudence, or "the Art of Life." Together these two concepts define Fielding's world of Order. As Providence is to the macrocosm, the universe at large, so is Prudence to the microcosm, man—the latter being that rational, pragmatic virtue that, in the moral sphere, is analogous to the Deity's wise and omniscient government of the creation. To a remarkable degree, the art of *Tom Jones* itself is the formal expression of these themes.

In Book X, Chapter i, Fielding applies to his novel a metaphor made familiar by Pope, Ralph Cudworth, and countless other philosophers or divines who saw the world as the work of a divine Artificer, a wise and benevolent Deity whose Word brought Order out of Chaos and whose careful providence conducts all men toward that final denouement in which the virtuous will be rewarded and the vicious punished. "This work," Fielding declares, "may, indeed, be considered as a great creation of our own; and for a little reptile of a critic to presume to find fault with any of its parts, without knowing the manner in which the whole is connected, and before he comes to the final catastrophe, is a most presumptuous absurdity." *Tom Jones* is a paradigm of the Augustan world view. Consider, for example, what may be called the "Palladian" architecture of the novel—that nice symmetry of structure by which the eighteen books of the novel are divided into three equal parts treating, respectively, the country, the journey, and the city, with the adventures at Upton forming the keystone of the arch at the mathematical center of the narrative and being balanced on either side by the digressions of the Man of the Hill and Mrs. Fitzpatrick. The design of *Tom Jones* mirrors a similar Order, a similar harmony and symmetry of parts, in Fielding's universe. Another, equally celebrated feature of the book, the omniscient narrator himself, functions, as both Thackeray and Wayne Booth have observed, as a kind of surrogate providence in the world of the novel, whose wit and wisdom we rely on and whose intrusions into the story keep us constantly aware of the shaping intelligence that arranges and governs all contingencies and will bring the characters at last to their just rewards. Though Professor Crane has brilliantly analyzed the "intricate scheme of probabilities" by which Fielding's plot develops organically, and though Fielding himself insists at length that the Probable is preferable to the Marvelous in fiction (VIII.i), it is no less true that many of the events in *Tom Jones* are the highly improbable contrivances of "Fortune." Tom's lucky encounter at the crossroads with the illiterate beggar who has found Sophia's lost pocketbook (XII.iv) is but one among many instances of the important role coincidence plays in the novel. As the divines whom Fielding read and admired were at pains to make clear, however, and as Tom Jones himself frequently acknowledges, it is Providence, not Fortune, that contrives the extraordinary casualties of life. The happy accidents and surprising reversals in Fielding's novel remind us of the manipulating intelligence of the author who conducts the story, as those in real life are signs of the Deity's providential care.

Chance, then, *is* Direction in the world of *Tom Jones,* as in the world celebrated in the *Essay on Man*. And the events in the novel ultimately lead toward a comic apocalypse—that last, improbable, joyous catastrophe in which true identities are discovered, the innocent redeemed, an unerring justice meted out to one and all. How is it, then, that one of the absurdities of *Pamela* that Fielding ridiculed was Richardson's insistence that virtue was rewarded in this world? "A very wholesome and comfortable doctrine," Fielding remarked in *Tom Jones* (XV.i), "and to which we have but one objection, namely, that it is not true." Why, one may well ask, should the happy conclusion of Fielding's own fiction be considered any less intellectually reprehensible than that of *Pamela?* The answer is implicit in what we have been saying so far about the relation of form to meaning in *Tom Jones*. Whereas Richardson offers *Pamela* to us as a literal transcription of reality, Fielding's intention is ultimately symbolic. In the preface to *Joseph Andrews,* Fielding saw the business of the comic novelist, as he saw that of his friend Hogarth, the "comic history-painter," as "the exactest copying of nature"; but he meant this in an Aristotelian, not a Baconian, sense. He would have agreed with Imlac in Johnson's *Rasselas* that the poet was not concerned to number the streaks of the tulip; his subject was "not men, but manners; not an individual, but a species." Richardson's eye is on the fact, Fielding's on the abstraction that the fact implies. The happy ending of *Pamela* is unacceptable because the novel asks to be taken as a faithful (even in a pious sense) representation of actuality. Fielding's fiction makes no such claim. Ultimately he asks us to consider not Tom Jones, but "HUMAN NATURE," not so much the particular story of one man's fall and redemption as that rational and benign scheme of things which the story and its witty, genial author imply. *Tom Jones* asks to be taken as a work of Art, as paradigm and emblem of that wise Design which Pope celebrated and in terms of which "partial Evil"—however real, however terrible—may be seen as "universal Good." The form of *Tom Jones*—its omniscient narrator and symmetrical design, its progression through probabilities and improbabilities to a fortunate conclusion—is the embodiment of its author's Christian vision: the vision of a world ordered and benign, and therefore "comic" in the profoundest sense.

The form of Fielding's masterpiece has, then, an ontological significance, the art of the novel implying the art of God. This, the assertion of Providence, is the book's implicit meaning; the recommendation of Prudence, "the Art of Life"—as Fielding, echoing Cicero, calls this virtue in *Amelia* (I.i)—is the explicit ethical purpose of the novel.[3] The word *prudence* (or the synonymous term *discretion*) recurs and reverberates throughout *Tom Jones*, acquiring something of the quality and function of a musical motif. But its meanings are curiously ambiguous: on the one hand, prudence is the summarizing vice of Blifil or Lady Bellaston, and on the other hand, prudence is that virtue Tom Jones must acquire before he reaches maturity as a moral agent. The problem for Tom, as for the reader, is to distinguish true prudence from false. It is a problem no less difficult than the definition of Wisdom itself.

In his dedication to Lyttelton, Fielding provides a clue to both the substance and the form of his major theme: invoking the Platonic metaphor comparing Virtue to a beautiful woman whose irresistible charms demand our love, he states that he intends not only to display "that beauty of virtue which may attract the admiration of mankind," but also to convince men "that their true interest directs them to a pursuit of her." The passage epitomizes the distinction familiar in the Christian humanist tradition between the two kinds of virtue or moral wisdom,

[3] For a full discussion of the theme of prudence and *sophia* in the novel, see my article "Fielding's Definition of Wisdom: Some Functions of Ambiguity and Emblem in *Tom Jones*," forthcoming in *ELH*, XXXV (1968).

sophia and *prudentia.* The apprehension of *sophia,* or speculative wisdom, was the goal of Plato's philosopher; the acquisition of *prudentia,* or practical wisdom, was the quest of Cicero's *vir honestus.* Prudence in this sense was the chief of the four cardinal virtues in antiquity. It is the ability, through the proper exercise of the rational faculties of memory, intelligence, and foresight, to distinguish truth from appearances and to estimate the future consequences of our present actions. It implies, furthermore, the power to choose between good and evil and to determine the right and effective means of achieving the one and of avoiding the other. This, as Allworthy observes, "is indeed the duty which we owe to ourselves" (XVIII.x). On the other hand, as it describes the less admirable characters in the novel—Blifil, Lady Bellaston, Deborah Wilkins, Jenny Jones, Mrs. Western, and Partridge, among a crowded gallery of the worldly and hypocritical—prudence reflects the modern definition of the term that had gained currency during the seventeenth century. Cicero had warned that cunning (*malitia*) was the counterfeit of wisdom (*prudentia*), and by Fielding's time, the popularity among middle-class readers of such works as Gracian's *The Art of Prudence* and William de Britaine's *Humane Prudence* had, in effect, transformed the supreme rational virtue of the ancients into that selfish and mean-spirited sense of expediency which the term now signifies. Robinson Crusoe and Pamela, the archetypal hero and heroine of the new bourgeois mythology, are "prudent" in this latter sense, the sagacity of the *vir honestus* having become, in Defoe and Richardson, the worldly wisdom of the *vir œconomicus.* Fielding's ambiguous use of prudence is calculated to test the reader's own ability to distinguish true from false, to involve us, as it were, in his hero's progress toward the acquisition of *prudentia.*

In this context the story of Tom Jones's disgrace and redemption, of his arduous journey toward reconciliation with his foster father and marriage with the woman he loves, takes on a broadly allegorical dimension; it is the story of our own deep need to live our lives with Wisdom. *Tom Jones* is not, of course, an allegory in the same sense or in the same way that *The Faerie Queene,* let us say, is an allegory. Fielding's novel differs from the conventional allegory in that its story is primary and autonomous. Characters, events, and setting have an integrity of their own and compel our interest in and for themselves; they do not require, at every point in the narrative, to be read off as signs and symbols in some controlling ideational system. Whereas Spenser's Una is "the One," Sophia Western is the girl Tom Jones loves and her family bullies. At the same time, however, within the world of the novel, Sophia is both cynosure and avatar—as her name implies, the center of the theme of Virtue and its incarnation. In her, to refer again to Fielding's use of the Platonic metaphor in his dedication, Virtue becomes "an object of sight." Similarly, though he is not of the same symbolic company as the Red Cross Knight or Bunyan's pilgrim, Tom Jones appears in the novel as a kind of Everyman striving toward maturity against his own weaknesses and the pressures of a hostile world.

Fielding's hero is possessed of every private and social virtue but one: he is honest, brave, and generous, but he is imprudent, and therefore imperfect as a moral agent. For want of prudence, Tom Jones is cast out of Paradise Hall, commits one good-natured indiscretion after another, and finds himself at last clapped into prison, rejected by Sophia and his foster father, and guilty (for all he knows) of incest and murder. After his expulsion from Paradise Hall, Tom's journey is at first aimless and uncertain: "*The world,* as Milton phrases it, *lay all before him*; and Jones, no more than Adam, had any man to whom he might resort for comfort or assistance" (VII.ii). After the crisis at Upton, however, when his mistress discovers his infidelity with Mrs. Waters, Tom's pursuit of Sophia will signify his gradual and painful attainment of *prudentia.* This, we recall, had been Fielding's purpose in writing the novel—to convince men "that their true interest directs them to a pursuit" of Virtue. In prison, at the nadir of his misfortunes, Tom Jones arrives at that crucial moment of self-awareness toward which the novel has been moving: "Sure . . . Fortune will never have done with me, 'till she hath driven me to distraction. But why do I blame Fortune? I am myself the cause of all my misery. All the dreadful mischiefs which have befallen me, are the consequences only of my own folly and vice" (XVIII.ii). At the moment when Fielding's hero confesses his folly and learns the lesson of prudence, the prison doors miraculously open, his "crimes" are undone, his enemies exposed, his true identity discovered. His marriage with Sophia follows inevitably. Within the frame of Fielding's comic vision of a just and ordered world, of a world in which Wisdom *is* attainable, it is the only possible conclusion.

Ideally, Fielding saw life as he saw art, not merely as energy, but as order. What he admired in men and in the natural world was a sort of benign exuberance rationally controlled and directed toward the attainment of a desirable end. The world of *Tom Jones* is dynamic, charged with the energy of sunshine and laughter and love. And it is at the same time a celebration of that rational design which gives meaning to vitality, and which alone, perhaps, makes it a source of joy and of wonder.

Tom Jones and "The Great Tradition": A Negative View

by F. R. Leavis

It is necessary to insist, then, that there are important distinctions to be made, and that far from all of the names in the literary histories really belong to the realm of significant creative achievement. And as a recall to a due sense of differences it is well to start by distinguishing the few really great—the major novelists who count in the same way as the major poets, in the sense that they not only change the possibilities of the art for practitioners and readers, but that they are significant in terms of the human awareness they promote, awareness of the possibilities of life.[1]

"Tom Jones and 'The Great Tradition': A Negative View" (Editor's title) by F. R. Leavis. From The Great Tradition: George Eliot, Henry James, Joseph Conrad (London: Chatto & Windus, Ltd., 1948; New York: New York University Press, 1963), pp. 2–4. Copyright 1948 by F. R. Leavis. Reprinted by permission of the author and publishers.

[1] Characteristic of the confusion I am contending against is the fashion (for which the responsibility seems to go back to Virginia Woolf and Mr. E. M. Forster) of talking of *Moll Flanders* as a "great novel." Defoe was a remarkable writer, but all that need be said about him as a novelist was said by Leslie Stephen in *Hours in a Library* (First Series). He made no pretension to practicing the novelist's art, and matters little as an influence. In fact, the only influence that need be noted is that represented by the use made of him in the nineteen-twenties by the practitioners of the fantastic *conte* (or pseudo-moral fable) with its empty pretense of significance. Associated with this use of Defoe is the use that was made in much the same *milieu* of Sterne, in whose irresponsible (and nasty) trifling, regarded as in some way extraordinarily significant and mature, was found a sanction for attributing value to other trifling.

The use of Bunyan by T. F. Powys is quite another matter. It is a mark of the genuine nature of Mr. Powys's creative gift (his work seems to me not to have had due recognition) that he has been able to achieve a kind of traditional relation to Bunyan—especially, of course, in *Mr. Weston's Good Wine*. Otherwise there is little that can be said with confidence about Bunyan as an influence. And yet we know him to have been for two centuries one of the most frequented of all classics, and in such a way that he counts immeasurably in the English-speaking consciousness. It is, perhaps, worth saying that his influence would tend strongly to reinforce the un-Flaubertian quality of the line of English classical fiction (Bunyan, Lord David Cecil

To insist on the pre-eminent few in this way is not to be indifferent to tradition; on the contrary, it is the way towards understanding what tradition is. "Tradition," of course, is a term with many forces—and often very little at all. There is a habit nowadays of suggesting that there is a tradition of "the English Novel," and that all that can be said of the tradition (that being its peculiarity) is that "the English Novel" can be anything you like. To distinguish the major novelists in the spirit proposed is to form a more useful idea of tradition (and to recognize that the conventionally established view of the past of English fiction needs to be drastically revised). It is in terms of the major novelists, those significant in the way suggested, that tradition, in any serious sense, has its significance.

To be important historically is not, of course, to be necessarily one of the significant few. Fielding deserves the place of importance given him in the literary histories, but he hasn't the kind of classical distinction we are also invited to credit him with. He is important not because he leads to Mr. J. B. Priestley but because he leads to Jane Austen, to appreciate whose distinction is to feel that life isn't long enough to permit of one's giving much time to Fielding or any to Mr. Priestley.

Fielding made Jane Austen possible by opening the central tradition of English fiction. In fact, to say that the English novel began with him is as reasonable as such propositions ever are. He completed the work begun by *The Tatler* and *The Spectator,* in the pages of which we see the drama turning into the novel—that this development should occur by way of journalism being in the natural course of things. To the art of presenting character and *mœurs* learnt in that school (he himself, before he became a novelist, was both playwright and periodical essayist) he joined a narrative habit the nature of which is sufficiently indicated by his own phrase, "comic epic in prose." That the eighteenth century, which hadn't much lively reading to choose from, but had much leisure, should have found *Tom Jones* exhilarating is not surprising; nor is it that Scott, and Coleridge, should have been able to give that work superlative praise. Standards are formed in comparison, and what opportunities had they for that? But the conventional talk about the "perfect construction" of *Tom Jones* (the late Hugh Walpole brought it out triumphantly and you may hear it in almost any course of lectures on "the English Novel") is absurd. There can't be subtlety of organization without richer matter to organize, and subtler interests, than Fielding has to offer. He is credited with range and variety and it is true that some episodes take place in the country and some in Town, some in the churchyard and some in the inn, some on the highroad and some in the bed-

---

might point out, was a Puritan), as well as to co-operate with the Jonsonian tradition of morally significant typicality in characters.

chamber, and so on. But we haven't to read a very large proportion of *Tom Jones* in order to discover the limits of the essential interests it has to offer us. Fielding's attitudes, and his concern with human nature, are simple, and not such as to produce an effect of anything but monotony (on a mind, that is, demanding more than external action) when exhibited at the length of an "epic in prose." What he *can* do appears to best advantage in *Joseph Andrews. Jonathan Wild,* with its famous irony, seems to me mere hobbledehoydom (much as one applauds the determination to explode the gangster-hero), and by *Amelia* Fielding has gone soft.

Fielding as Novelist: *Tom Jones*

by Ian Watt

On further analysis, then, it appears that Johnson's comparison between Richardson and Fielding does not directly raise the question of which was the better psychologist, but depends rather on their quite opposite literary intentions: those of Fielding allotted characterization a much less important place in his total literary structure, and precluded him even from attempting the effects which were suited to Richardson's very different aim. The full implications of the divergence can perhaps be most clearly and inclusively demonstrated in Fielding's handling of the plot in *Tom Jones,* for it reflects the whole of his social, moral, and literary outlook.

Fielding's conduct of the action, despite a few excrescences such as the interpolated story of the Man of the Hill, and some signs of haste and confusion in the concluding books,[1] exhibits a remarkably fine control over a very complicated structure, and abundantly justifies Coleridge's famous eulogy: "What a master of composition Fielding was! Upon my word, I think the *Oedipus Tyrannus,* the *Alchemist,* and *Tom Jones,* the three most perfect plots ever planned." [2]

Perfect for what? we must ask. Not, certainly, for the exploration of character and of personal relations, since in all three plots the emphasis falls on the author's skilfully contrived revelation of an external and deterministic scheme: in *Oedipus* the hero's character is of minor importance compared with the consequences of his past actions, which were themselves the result of a prophecy made long before his birth; in the *Alchemist* the portrayal of Face and Subtle does not go far beyond the need for suitable instruments to carry out Jonson's complex series of

"Fielding as Novelist" by Ian Watt. From sections ii and iv, Chapter IX (*"Fielding as Novelist:* Tom Jones"), *of* The Rise of the Novel: Studies in Defoe, Richardson, and Fielding *(Berkeley and Los Angeles: University of California Press, 1957; London: Chatto & Windus, Ltd., 1957), pp. 268–80, 285–89. Copyright © 1957 by Chatto & Windus, Ltd. Reprinted by permission of the author and publishers.*

[1] For a full account see F. H. Dudden, *Henry Fielding,* II, 621–627.
[2] F. T. Blanchard, *Fielding the Novelist,* pp. 320f.

chicaneries; while the plot of *Tom Jones* offers a combination of these features. As in Sophocles, the crucial secret, that of the hero's actual birth, is very elaborately prepared for and hinted at throughout the action, and its eventual disclosure brings about the final reordering of all the main issues of the story: while, as in Jonson, this final reordering is achieved through the unmasking of a complicated pattern of villainy and deception.

The three plots are alike in another respect: their basic direction is towards a return to the norm, and they therefore have a fundamentally static quality. In this they no doubt reflect the conservatism of their authors, a conservatism which in Fielding's case is probably connected with the fact that he belonged, not to the trading class like Defoe and Richardson, but to the gentry. The plots of the novels of Defoe and Richardson, as we have seen, mirrored certain dynamic tendencies in the outlook of their class: in *Moll Flanders,* for example, money has a certain autonomous force which determines the action at every turn. In *Tom Jones,* on the other hand, as in the *Alchemist,* money is something that the good characters either have or are given or momentarily lose: only bad characters devote any effort either to getting it or keeping it. Money, in fact, is a useful plot device but it has no controlling significance.

Birth, on the other hand, has a very different status in *Tom Jones:* as a determining factor in the plot it is almost the equivalent of money in Defoe or virtue in Richardson. In this emphasis, of course, Fielding reflects the general tenor of the social thought of his day: the basis of society is and should be a system of classes each with their own capacities and responsibilities. The vigor of Fielding's satire on the upper classes, for example, should not be interpreted as the expression of any egalitarian tendency: it is really a tribute to the firmness of his belief in the class premise. It is true that in *Amelia* he goes so far as to say that "of all kinds of pride, there is none so unchristian as that of station." [3] But that, of course, is only a matter of *noblesse oblige;* and in *Tom Jones* Fielding also wrote that "liberality of spirits" was a quality which he had "scarce ever seen in men of low birth and education." [4]

This class fixity is an essential part of *Tom Jones.* Tom may think it unfortunate that, as a foundling of presumed low ancestry, he cannot marry Sophia; but he does not question the propriety of the assumption on which their separation is decreed. The ultimate task of Fielding's plot therefore is to unite the lovers without subverting the basis of the social order; and this can only be done by revealing that Mr. Jones, though illegitimate, is genteel. This, however, is not wholly a surprise to the perceptive reader, for whom Tom's eminent "liberality of spirit" has already suggested his superior pedigree; the recent Soviet critic, therefore,

---

[3] Bk. VII, ch. 10.
[4] Bk. IX, ch. 1. See also A. O. Lovejoy, *The Great Chain of Being* (Harvard, 1936), pp. 224, 245.

who sees the story as the triumph of a proletarian hero[5] is neglecting, not only the facts of his birth, but its continuing implications for his character.

Fielding's conservatism accounts for another and much more general difference between the plots of *Tom Jones* and *Clarissa:* for whereas Richardson depicts the crucifixion of the individual by society, Fielding portrays the successful adaptation of the individual to society, and this entails a very different relation between plot and character.

In *Clarissa* the individual must be given priority in the total structure: Richardson merely brings together certain individuals, and their proximity is all that is necessary to set off an extended chain reaction which then proceeds under its own impetus and modifies all the characters and their mutual relationships. In *Tom Jones,* on the other hand, society and the larger order which it represents must have priority, and the plot's function, therefore, is to perform a physical rather than a chemical change: it acts as a kind of magnet that pulls every individual particle out of the random order brought about by temporal accident and human imperfection and puts them all back into their proper position. The constitution of the particles themselves—the characters—is not modified in the process, but the plot serves to reveal something much more important—the fact that all human particles are subject to an ultimate invisible force which exists in the universe whether they are there to show it or not.

Such a plot reflects the general literary strategy of neo-classicism; just as the creation of a field of force makes visible the universal laws of magnetism, so the supreme task of the writer was to make visible in the human scene the operations of universal order—to unveil the handiwork of Pope's "Unerring Nature, still divinely bright,/One clear, unchanged and universal light."

This much wider perspective on character obviously reduces the importance which will be attached to the nature and actions of any particular individual entity—they are mainly interesting as manifestations of the great pattern of Nature. This informs Fielding's treatment of every aspect of characterization—not only the extent to which his *dramatis personae* are individualized, but the degree of attention paid to their subjective lives, to their moral development, and to their personal relationships.

Fielding's primary objectives in the portrayal of character are clear but limited: to assign them to their proper category by giving as few diagnostic features as are necessary for the task. Such was his conception of "invention" or "creation": "a quick and sagacious penetration into the true essence of all the objects of our contemplation." [6] This meant

[5] A. Elistratov, "Fielding's Realism," in *Iz Istorii Angliskogo Realizma* [On the History of English Realism] (Moscow, 1941), p. 63.
[6] Bk. IX, ch. 1.

in practice that once the individual had been appropriately labeled the author's only remaining duty was to see that he continued to speak and act consistently. As Aristotle put it in the *Poetics,* "character" is "that which reveals the moral purpose," and consequently "speeches . . . which do not make this manifest . . . are not expressive of character." [7] Parson Supple must never cease to be supple.

So it is that Fielding does not make any attempt to individualize his characters. Allworthy is sufficiently categorized by his name, while that of Tom Jones, compounded as it is out of two of the commonest names in the language, tells us that we must regard him as the representative of manhood in general, in accordance with his creator's purpose to show "not men, but manners; not an individual, but a species." [8]

The scope of the word *manners* has dwindled so drastically in the last few centuries—no doubt as a result of the way individualism has reduced the areas in which identity of thought and action is generally expected— that the phrase "characters of manners" no longer means very much. It can perhaps be best explained in terms of the contrast with Richardson's "characters of nature." Richardson's literary objective, as B. W. Downs has pointed out,[9] is not so much character—the stable elements in the individual's mental and moral constitution—as personality: he does not analyze Clarissa, but presents a complete and detailed behavioral report on her whole being: she is defined by the fullness of our participation in her life. Fielding's purpose, on the other hand, is analytic: he is not interested in the exact configuration of motives in any particular person's mind at any particular time but only in those features of the individual which are necessary to assign him to his moral and social species. He therefore studies each character in the light of his general knowledge of human behavior, of "manners," and anything purely individual is of no taxonomic value. Nor is there any need to look inside: if, as Johnson said, Fielding gives us the husk, it is because the surface alone is usually quite sufficient to identify the specimen—the expert does not need to assay the kernel.

There are many other reasons for Fielding's predominantly external approach to character, reasons of a social and philosophical as well as of a literary order. To begin with, the opposite approach involved a breach of decorum: as Fielding's cousin Lady Mary Wortley Montagu pointed out, it was very bad manners for Richardson's heroines to "declare all they think," since "fig leaves are as necessary for our minds as our bodies." [10] It was also consistent with the classical tradition as a whole, as we have seen, to avoid the intimate and confessional approach to person-

---

[7] Ch. 6, No. 17.
[8] *Joseph Andrews,* Bk. III, ch. 1.
[9] *Richardson,* pp. 125f.
[10] *Letters and Works,* II, 291.

ality; and in any case the philosophical problems of self-consciousness
had only begun to receive attention some six centuries after Aristotle in
the works of Plotinus.[11] Lastly, as was evident in the treatment of Blifil
and Sophia, Fielding's comic purpose itself required an external approach, and for a compelling reason. If we identify ourselves with the
characters, we shall not be in any mood to appreciate the humor of the
larger comedy in which they are risible participants: life, we have been
told, is a comedy only to the man who thinks, and the comic author
must not make us feel every stroke of the lash as his characters squirm
under his corrective rod.

At all events, Fielding avowedly and even ostentatiously refused to go
too deep into the minds of his characters, on the general grounds that
"it is our province to relate facts, and we shall leave causes to persons
of much higher genius." We have noted how little was said about the
feelings, as opposed to the rational determinations, of Blifil and Sophia.
This was quite conscious on Fielding's part: he had already remarked
ironically of Blifil that "it would be an ill office in us to pay a visit to the
inmost recesses of his mind, as some scandalous people search into the
most secret affairs of their friends, and often pry into their closets and
cupboards, only to discover their poverty and meanness to the world";
similarly when Fielding came to present Sophia's feelings when she first
learned of Tom's love, he excused himself in the words: "as to the present situation of her mind I shall adhere to the rule of Horace, by not
attempting to describe it, from despair of success." [12]

Fielding's avoidance of the subjective dimension, then, is quite inten-
tional: but that does not, of course, mean that it has no drawbacks, for
it undoubtedly has, and they become very apparent whenever important
emotional climaxes are reached. Coleridge, for all his love of Fielding,
pointed out that in the soliloquies between Sophia and Tom Jones before their final reconciliation, nothing could be "more forced and unnatural: the language is without vivacity or spirit, the whole matter is
incongruous, and totally devoid of psychological truth." [13] In fact, Fielding merely gave us a stock comic scene: elevated sentiments of penitent
ardor on the hero's part were countered by wronged womanhood's
equally elevated scorn of her faithless suitor. Soon after, of course,
Sophia accepts Tom, and we are surprised by her very sudden and un-
explained reversal: the denouement has been given a certain comic life,
but at the expense of the reality of emotions involved.

This emotional artificiality is very general in *Tom Jones.* When the
hero, for instance, is expelled from Allworthy's house we are told that
". . . he presently fell into the most violent agonies, tearing his hair

[11] See A. E. Taylor, *Aristotle* (London, 1943), p. 108.
[12] Bk. II, ch. 4; Bk. IV, chs. 3, 14.
[13] Blanchard, *Fielding,* p. 317.

from his head, and using most other actions which generally accompany fits of madness, rage and despair"; and later that he read Sophia's parting letter "a hundred times over, and kissed it a hundred times as often." [14] Fielding's use of these hackneyed hyperboles to vouch for the intensity of the emotions of his characters underlines the price that he pays for his comic approach: it denies him a convincing and continuous access to the inner life of his characters, so that whenever he has to exhibit their emotional life, he can only do it externally by making them have exaggerated physical reactions.

The fact that Fielding's characters do not have a convincing inner life means that their possibilities of psychological development are very limited. Tom Jones's character, for example, exhibits some development, but it is of a very general kind. Tom's early imprudences, his youthful lack of worldly wisdom, and his healthy animality, for example, lead to his disgrace, his expulsion from the Allworthy household, his subsequent difficulties on the road and in London, and his apparently irrecoverable loss of Sophia's love. At the same time his good qualities, his courage, honor, and benevolence, all of which have been glimpsed at the beginning, eventually combine to extricate him from the nadir of his misfortunes, and restore him to the love and respect of those who surround him. But although different qualities come to the fore at different times, they have all been present from the beginning, and we have not been taken close enough to Tom's mind to be able to do anything but take on trust Fielding's implication, which is that his hero will be able to control his weaknesses by the wisdom he has learned of experience.

In taking this essentially static view of human nature Fielding was following the time-hallowed Aristotelian view, which was actually held with much greater rigidity by most of the philosophers and literary critics of his time.[15] It is, of course, an a-historical view of character, as Fielding showed in *Joseph Andrews,* when he asserted that his characters were "taken from the life," but added that the particular lawyer in question was "not only alive, but hath been so these four thousand years." [16] It follows logically that if human nature is essentially stable, there is no need to detail the processes whereby any one example of it has reached its full development; such processes are but temporary and superficial modifications of a moral constitution which is unalterably fixed from birth. Such, for example, is the premise of the way that although Tom and Blifil share the same mother and are brought up in the same household by the same tutors, their respective courses are unalterably set in different directions from the very beginning.

[14] Bk. VI, ch. 12.
[15] See Leslie Stephen, *English Thought in the Eighteenth Century* (London, 1902), II, 73f.; R. Hubert, *Les Sciences sociales dans l'Encyclopédie* (Paris, 1923), pp. 167ff.
[16] Bk. III, ch. 1.

Once again the contrast with Richardson is complete. Much of our sense of Clarissa's psychological development arises from the way that her experience brings a continual deepening of her understanding of her own past: as a result character and plot are indivisible. Tom Jones, on the other hand, is not in touch with his own past at all: we feel a certain unreality in his actions because they always seem to be spontaneous reactions to stimuli that the plot has been manipulated to provide; we have no sense that they are manifestations of a developing moral life. We cannot but feel surprise, for instance, when, immediately after accepting 50 pounds from Lady Bellaston, Tom gives his famous lecture to Nightingale on sexual ethics.[17] It is not that the two actions are inherently contradictory—Tom's ethics have throughout been based on the much greater heinousness of harming others than of failing to live up to one's moral code oneself; but if we had been given some indication that Tom was aware of the apparent contradictions between his speech and his own past practice, he might have sounded less priggish and more convincing. Actually, of course, separate parts of Tom's nature can hold very little converse with each other, because there is only one agency for such converse —the individual consciousness through which the whole repertoire of past actions operates—and Fielding does not take us into this consciousness because he believes that individual character is a specific combination of stable and separate predispositions to action, rather than the product of its own past.

For the same reasons personal relationships are also relatively unimportant in *Tom Jones*. If there is a controlling force independent of the individual actors and their positions with respect to each other, and if their own characters are innate and unchanging, there is no reason why Fielding should give close attention to their mutual feelings, since they cannot play a decisive role. Here, again, the scene between Sophia and Blifil was typical in that it reflected the extent to which the structure of *Tom Jones* as a whole depends on the lack of any effective communication between the characters: just as Blifil must misunderstand Sophia, so Allworthy must fail to see Blifil in his true light, and Tom must be unable either to understand Blifil's true nature or to explain himself properly either to Allworthy or Sophia until the closing scenes. For, since Fielding's view of human life and his general literary purpose did not permit him to subordinate his plot to the deepening exploration of personal relationships, he needed a structure based on an elaborate counterpoint of deception and surprise, and this would be impossible if the characters could share each other's minds and take their fates into their own hands.

[17] Bk. XIV, ch. 7.

There is, then, an absolute connection in *Tom Jones* between the treatment of plot and of character. Plot has priority, and it is therefore plot which must contain the elements of complication and development. Fielding achieves this by superimposing on a central action that is, in essentials as simple as that in *Clarissa,* a very complex series of relatively autonomous subplots and episodes which are in the nature of dramatic variations on the main theme. These relatively independent narrative units are combined in a concatenation whose elaboration and symmetry is suggested in the most obvious outward aspect of the book's formal order: unlike the novels of Defoe and Richardson, *Tom Jones* is carefully divided into compositional units of different sizes—some two hundred chapters which are themselves grouped into eighteen books disposed into three groups of six, dealing respectively with the early lives, the journeys to London, and the activities on arrival, of the main characters.

This extreme diversification of the narrative texture reinforces, of course, Fielding's tendency not to dwell for long on any one scene or character. In the passages quoted, for example, there was none of the intensive treatment which Richardson gave to Clarissa's interview with Solmes; most of Fielding's time was spent on making clear the initial misunderstanding, and the scale of the scene allowed no more in the way of characterization than a designing hypocrite, a trapped maiden, and a heavy father. But even if there had been any full absorption in the feelings of Sophia, for example, it would soon have been terminated by the management of the ensuing scenes: for, just as we left Sophia immediately after Squire Western had stormed out of the room, and were thus spared any prolonged awareness of her sufferings, so in the next chapter our attention was soon switched away from her parting interview with Tom Jones by Fielding's announcement that ". . . the scene, which I believe some of my readers will think had lasted long enough, was interrupted by one of so different a nature, that we shall reserve the relation of it for a different chapter." [18]

This is typical of the narrative mode of *Tom Jones*: the author's commentary makes no secret of the fact that his aim is not to immerse us wholly in his fictional world, but rather to show the ingenuity of his own inventive resources by contriving an amusing counterpoint of scenes and characters; quick changes are the essence of Fielding's comic manner, and a new chapter will always bring a new situation for the characters, or present different characters in a similar scene for ironical contrast. In addition, by a great variety of devices, of which the chapter headings are usually significant pointers, our attention is continually drawn to the fact that the ultimate cohesive force of the book resides not in the charac-

[18] Bk. VI, ch. 8.

ters and their relationships, but in an intellectual and literary structure which has a considerable degree of autonomy.

The effects of this procedure and its relationship to Fielding's treatment of character can be summarized in relation to a brief scene which occurs after Tom has heard that Allworthy is to recover from his illness. He takes a walk "in a most delicious grove," and contemplates the cruelty of fortune which separates him from his beloved Sophia:

> Was I but possessed of thee, one only suit of rags thy whole estate, is there a man on earth whom I would envy! How contemptible would the brightest Circassian beauty, dressed in all the jewels of the Indies, appear to my eyes! But why do I mention another woman? Could I think my eyes capable of looking at any other with tenderness, these hands should tear them from my head. No, my Sophia, if cruel fortune separates us forever, my soul shall dote on thee alone. The chastest constancy will I ever preserve to thy image . . .
>
> At these words he started up and beheld—not his Sophia—no, nor a Circassian maid richly and elegantly attired for the grand Signior's seraglio . . .

but Molly Seagrim, with whom, "after a parley" which Fielding omits, Tom retires to "the thickest part of the grove." [19]

The least convincing aspect of the episode is the diction: the speech habits manifested here obviously bear little relation to those we expect of Tom Jones. But, of course, they are a stylistic necessity for Fielding's immediate purpose—the comic deflation of the heroic and romantic pretenses of the human word by the unheroic and unromantic eloquence of the human deed. Tom Jones is no more than a vehicle for the expression of Fielding's scepticism about lovers' vows; and he must be made to speak in terms that parody the high-flown rhetoric of the pastoral romance to give point to the succeeding wayside encounter which belongs to the very different world of the *pastourelle*. Nor can Fielding pause to detail the psychological processes whereby Tom is metamorphosed from Sophia's romantic lover to Moll's prompt gallant: to illustrate the commonplace that "actions speak louder than words," the actions must be very silent and they must follow very hard upon very loud words.

The relation of this episode to the larger structure of the novel is typical. One of Fielding's general organizing themes is the proper place of sex in human life; this encounter neatly illustrates the conflicting tendencies of headstrong youth, and shows that Tom has not yet reached the continence of moral adulthood. The scene, therefore, plays its part in the general moral and intellectual scheme; and it is also significantly connected with the workings of the plot, since Tom's lapse eventually becomes a factor in his dismissal by Allworthy, and therefore leads to the ordeals which eventually make him a worthier mate for Sophia.

[19] Bk. V, ch. 10.

At the same time Fielding's treatment of the scene is also typical in avoiding any detailed presentation of Tom's feelings either at the time or later—to take his hero's faithlessness too seriously would jeopardize Fielding's primarily comic intention in the episode, and he therefore manipulates it in such a way as to discourage us from giving it a significance which it might have in ordinary life. Comedy, and especially comedy on an elaborate scale, often involves this kind of limited liability to psychological interpretation: it applies to Blifil's malice and to Sophia's sufferings in the scenes quoted earlier, and Allworthy's sudden illness and recovery, which have led to Tom's lapse, must be placed in the same perspective. We must not dwell on the apparent fact that Allworthy is incapable of distinguishing between a cold and a mortal illness, since we are not intended to draw the implications for his character that he is either an outrageous hypochondriac or lamentably unskilled in choosing physicians: Allworthy's illness is only a diplomatic chill, and we must not infer anything from it except a shift in Fielding's narrative policy.

Tom Jones, then, would seem to exemplify a principle of considerable significance for the novel form in general: namely, that the importance of the plot is in inverse proportion to that of character. This principle has an interesting corollary: the organization of the narrative into an extended and complex formal structure will tend to turn the protagonists into its passive agents, but it will offer compensatingly greater opportunities for the introduction of a variety of minor characters, whose treatment will not be hampered in the same way by the roles which they are allotted by the complications of the narrative design.

The principle and its corollary would seem to lie behind Coleridge's contrast of the "forced and unnatural quality" of the scenes between the protagonists in *Tom Jones* and Fielding's treatment of the "characters of postilions, landlords, landladies, waiters" where "nothing can be more true, more happy or more humorous." [20] These minor characters figure only in scenes which require exactly the amount of psychological individuality which they are possessed of; relieved of any responsibility for carrying out the major narrative design Mrs. Honour can get herself dismissed from the Western household by methods which are at once triumphantly comic, sociologically perceptive, and eminently characteristic;[21] nor is there any question of the violence to character and probability which colors the ways whereby Tom Jones, for example, or Sophia leave home.

Such is the pattern of most comic novels with elaborate plots, from Fielding and Smollett to Dickens: the creative emphasis is on characters

---

[20] Blanchard, *Fielding,* p. 317.
[21] Bk. VII, ch. 7.

who are minor at least in the sense that they are not deeply involved in the working out of the plot; whereas the Tom Jones's, the Roderick Randoms and the David Copperfields are less convincing as characters because their personalities bear little direct relation to the part they must play, and some of the actions in which the plot involves them suggest a weakness or folly which is probably at variance with the actual intentions of their author towards them.

On the other hand, the type of novel which is perhaps most typical of the genre, and which achieves effects which have not been duplicated in any other literary form, has used a very different kind of plot. From Sterne and Jane Austen to Proust and Joyce the Aristotelian priority of plot over character has been wholly reversed, and a new type of formal structure has been evolved in which the plot attempts only to embody the ordinary processes of life and in so doing becomes wholly dependent on the characters and the development of their relationships. It is Defoe and above all Richardson who provide this tradition with its archetypes, just as it is Fielding who provides that for the opposite tradition.

*   *   *

As far as most modern readers are concerned it is not Fielding's moral but his literary point of view which is open to objection. For his conception of his role is that of a guide who, not content with taking us "behind the scenes of this great theatre of nature," [22] feels that he must explain everything which is to be found there; and such authorial intrusion, of course, tends to diminish the authenticity of his narrative.

Fielding's personal intrusion into *Tom Jones* begins with his dedication to the Honorable George Lyttelton, a dedication, it must be admitted, which goes far to justify Johnson's definition of this form of writing—"a servile address to a patron." There are numerous further references in the body of his work to others among Fielding's patrons, notably Ralph Allen and Lord Chancellor Hardwicke, not to mention other acquaintances whom Fielding wished to compliment, including one of his surgeons, Mr. John Ranby, and various innkeepers.

The effect of these references is certainly to break the spell of the imaginary world represented in the novel: but the main interference with the autonomy of this world comes from Fielding's introductory chapters, containing literary and moral essays, and even more from his frequent discussions and asides to the reader within the narrative itself. There is no doubt that Fielding's practice here leads him in completely the opposite direction from Richardson, and converts the novel into a social and indeed into a sociable literary form. Fielding brings us into a charmed circle composed, not only of the fictional characters, but also of Fielding's friends and of his favorites among the poets and moralists of the past.

[22] Bk. VII, ch. 1.

He is, indeed, almost as attentive to his audience as to his characters, and his narrative, far from being an intimate drama which we peep at through a keyhole, is a series of reminiscences told by a genial raconteur in some wayside inn—the favored and public locus of his tale.

This approach to the novel is quite consistent with Fielding's major intention—it promotes a distancing effect which prevents us from being so fully immersed in the lives of the characters that we lose our alertness to the larger implications of their actions—implications which Fielding brings out in his capacity of omniscient chorus. On the other hand, Fielding's interventions obviously interfere with any sense of narrative illusion, and break with almost every narrative precedent, beginning with that set by Homer, whom Aristotle praised for saying "very little *in propria persona*," and for maintaining elsewhere the attitude either of a dispassionate narrator, or of an impersonator of one of the characters.[23]

Few readers would like to be without the prefatory chapters, or Fielding's diverting asides, but they undoubtedly derogate from the reality of the narrative: as Richardson's friend, Thomas Edwards, wrote, "we see every moment" that it is Fielding who "does *personam gerere*," whereas Richardson is "the thing itself." [24] So, although Fielding's garrulity about his characters and his conduct of the action initiated a popular practice in the English novel; it is not surprising that it has been condemned by most modern critics, and on these grounds. Ford Madox Ford, for instance, complained that the "trouble with the English nuvvelist from Fielding to Meredith, is that not one of them cares whether you believe in their characters or not";[25] and Henry James was shocked by the way Trollope, and other "accomplished novelists," concede "in a digression, a parenthesis or an aside" that their fiction is "only make-believe." James went on to lay down the central principle of the novelist's attitude to his creation, which is very similar to that described above as inherent in formal realism: Trollope, and any novelist who shares his attitude, James says,

> admits that the events he narrates have not really happened, and that he can give the narrative any turn the reader may like best. Such a betrayal of a sacred office seems to me, I confess, a terrible crime; it is what I mean by the attitude of apology, and it shocks me every whit as much in Trollope as it would have shocked me in Gibbon or Macaulay. It implies that the novelist is less occupied in looking for the truth (the truth of course I mean, that he assumes, the premises that we must grant him, whatever they may be) than the historian, and in so doing it deprives him at a stroke of all his standing room.[26]

[23] *Poetics*, chs. 24, 3.
[24] A. D. McKillop, *Samuel Richardson* (Chapel Hill, 1936), p. 175.
[25] *English Novel*, p. 89.
[26] "The Art of Fiction" (1884); cited from *The Art of Fiction*, ed. Bishop, p. 5.

There is not, of course, any doubt as to Fielding's intention of "looking for the truth"—he tells us indeed in *Tom Jones* that "we determined to guide our pen throughout by the directions of truth." But he perhaps underestimated the connection between truth and the maintenance of the reader's "historical faith." This, at least, is the suggestion of a passage towards the end of *Tom Jones* when he proclaims that he will let his hero be hanged rather than extricate him from his troubles by unnatural means "for we had rather relate that he was hanged at Tyburn (which may very probably be the case) than forfeit our integrity, or shock the faith of our reader." [27]

This ironical attitude towards the reality of his creation was probably responsible in part for the main critical doubt which *Tom Jones* suggests. It is, in the main, a very true book, but it is by no means so clear that its truth has, to quote R. S. Crane, been "rendered" in terms of the novel.[28] We do not get the impressive sense of Fielding's own moral qualities from his characters or their actions that we do from the heroic struggles for human betterment which he conducted as a magistrate under the most adverse personal circumstances, or even from the *Journal of a Voyage to Lisbon*; and if we analyze our impression from the novels alone it surely is evident that our residual impression of dignity and generosity comes mainly from the passages where Fielding is speaking in his own person. And this, surely, is the result of a technique which was deficient at least in the sense that it was unable to convey this larger moral significance through character and action alone, and could only supply it by means of a somewhat intrusive patterning of the plot and by direct editorial commentary. As Henry James put it: Tom Jones "has so much 'life' that it amounts, for the effect of comedy and application of satire, almost to his having a mind"; almost, but not quite, and so it was necessary that "his author—*he* handsomely possessed of a mind—[should have] such an amplitude of reflection for him and round him that we see him through the mellow air of Fielding's fine old moralism. . . ." [29]

All this, of course, is not to say Fielding does not succeed: *Tom Jones* is surely entitled to the praise of an anonymous early admirer who called it "on the whole . . . the most lively book ever published." [30] But it is a very personal and unrepeatable kind of success: Fielding's technique was too eclectic to become a permanent element in the tradition of the novel—*Tom Jones* is only part novel, and there is much else—picaresque tale, comic drama, occasional essay.

[27] Bk. III, ch. 1; Bk. XVII, ch. 1.
[28] "The Concept of Plot and the Plot of *Tom Jones*," *Critics and Criticism Ancient and Modern* (Chicago, 1952), p. 639. [See p. 68 of this volume.]
[29] Preface, *The Princess Casamassima*.
[30] *Essay on the New Species of Writing Founded by Mr. Fielding* (1751), p. 43.

On the other hand, Fielding's departure from the canons of formal realism indicated very clearly the nature of the supreme problem which the new genre had to face. The tedious asseveration of literal authenticity in Defoe and to some extent in Richardson, tended to obscure the fact that, if the novel was to achieve equality of status with other genres it had to be brought into contact with the whole tradition of civilized values, and supplement its realism of presentation with a realism of assessment. To the excellent Mrs. Barbauld's query as to the grounds on which he considered Richardson to be a lesser writer than Shakespeare, Coleridge answered that "Richardson is *only* interesting." [31] This is no doubt unfair as a total judgment on the author of *Clarissa,* but it indicates the likely limits of a realism of presentation: we shall be wholly immersed in the reality of the characters and their actions, but whether we shall be any wiser as a result is open to question.

Fielding brought to the genre something that is ultimately even more important than narrative technique—a responsible wisdom about human affairs which plays upon the deeds and the characters of his novels. His wisdom is not, perhaps, of the highest order; it is, like that of his beloved Lucian, a little inclined to be easygoing and on occasion opportunist. Nevertheless, at the end of *Tom Jones* we feel we have been exposed, not merely to an interesting narrative about imaginary persons, but to a stimulating wealth of suggestion and challenge on almost every topic of human interest. Not only so: the stimulation has come from a mind with a true grasp of human reality, never deceived or deceiving about himself, his characters, or the human lot in general. In his effort to infuse the new genre with something of the Shakespearean virtues Fielding departed too far from formal realism to initiate a viable tradition, but his work serves as a perpetual reminder that if the new genre was to challenge older literary forms it had to find a way of conveying not only a convincing impression but a wise assessment of life, an assessment that could only come from taking a much wider view than Defoe or Richardson of the affairs of mankind.

So, although we must agree with the tenor of Johnson's watch simile, we must also add that it is unfair and misleading. Richardson, no doubt, takes us deeper into the inner workings of the human machine; but Fielding is surely entitled to retort that there are many other machines in nature besides the individual consciousness, and perhaps to express his surprised chagrin that Johnson should apparently have overlooked the fact that he was engaged in the exploration of a vaster and equally intricate mechanism, that of human society as a whole, a literary subject which was, incidentally, much more consonant than Richardson's with the classical outlook which he and Johnson shared.

[31] Blanchard, *Fielding,* p. 316.

Tom Jones

by William Empson

I had been meaning to write about *Tom Jones* before, but this essay bears the marks of shock at what I found said about the book by recent literary critics, and my students at Sheffield; I had to consider why I find the book so much better than they do. Middleton Murry was working from the same impulse of defense in the chief of the *Unprofessional Essays* (1956) written shortly before he died; I agree with him so much that we chose a lot of the same quotations, but he was still thinking of Fielding as just "essentially healthy" or something like that, and I think the defense should be larger. Of American critics, I remember a detailed treatment of the plot by a Chicago Aristotelian, who praised what may be called the calculations behind the structure; I thought this was just and sensible, but assumed the basic impulse behind the book to be pretty trivial. English critics tend to bother about *Tom Jones* more than American ones and also to wince away from it more, because it is supposed to be so frightfully English, and they are rightly uneasy about national self-praise; besides, he is hearty and they tend to be anti-hearty. What nobody will recognize, I feel, is that Fielding set out to preach a doctrine in *Tom Jones* (1749), and said so, a high-minded though perhaps abstruse one. As he said after the attacks on *Joseph Andrews* (1742) that he would not write another novel, we may suppose that he wouldn't have written *Tom Jones* without at least finding for himself the excuse that he had this important further thing to say. Modern critics tend to assume both (a) that it isn't artistic to preach any doctrine and (b) that the only high-minded doctrine to preach is despair and contempt for the world; I think the combination produces a critical blind spot, so I hope there is some general interest in this attempt to defend *Tom Jones*, even for those who would not mark the book high anyhow.

Fielding, then, is regarded with a mixture of acceptance and contempt, as a worthy old boy who did the basic engineering for the novel because he invented the clockwork plot, but tiresomely boisterous, "broad" to

"Tom Jones" *by William Empson. From* The Kenyon Review, XX *(1958), 217–49. Copyright* © *1958 by* The Kenyon Review. *Reprinted by permission of the author and publishers.*

the point of being insensitive to fine shades, lacking in any of the higher aspirations, and hampered by a style which keeps his prosy common-sense temperament always to the fore. Looking for a way out of this clump of prejudices, I think the style is the best place to start. If you take an interest in Fielding's opinions, which he seems to be expressing with bluff directness, you can get to the point of reading *Tom Jones* with fascinated curiosity, baffled to make out what he really does think about the filial duties of a daughter, or the inherent virtues of a gentle-man, or the Christian command of chastity. To leap to ambiguity for a solution may seem Empson's routine paradox, particularly absurd in the case of Fielding; but in a way, which means for a special kind of ambiguity, it has always been recognized about him. His readers have always felt sure that he is somehow recommending the behavior of Tom Jones, whether they called the result healthy or immoral; whereas the book makes plenty of firm assertions that Tom is doing wrong. The reason why this situation can arise is that the style of Fielding is a habitual double irony; or rather, he moves the gears of his car up to that as soon as the road lets it use its strength. This form, though logically rather complicated, needs a show of lightness and carelessness whether it is being used to cheat or not; for that matter, some speakers convey it all the time by a curl of the tongue in their tone of voice. Indeed, I understand that some Americans regard every upper-class English voice as doing that, however unintentionally; to divide the na-tional honors, I should think the reason for the suspicion is that every tough American voice is doing it too. Single irony presumes a censor; the ironist (A) is fooling a tyrant (B) while appealing to the judgment of a person addressed (C). For double irony A shows both B and C that he understands both their positions; B can no longer forbid direct utter-ance, but I think can always be picked out as holding the more official or straight-faced belief. In real life this is easier than single irony (be-cause people aren't such fools as you think), so that we do not always notice its logical structure. Presumably A hopes that each of B and C will think "He is secretly on my side, and only pretends to sympathize with the other"; but A may hold some wise balanced position between them, or contrariwise may be feeling "a plague on both your houses." The trick is liable to be unpopular, and perhaps literary critics despise its evasiveness, so that when they talk about irony they generally seem to mean something else; but a moderate amount of it is felt to be bal-anced and unfussy. The definition may seem too narrow, but if you generalize the term to cover almost any complex state of mind it ceases to be useful. I do not want to make large claims for "double irony," but rather to narrow it down enough to show why it is peculiarly fitted for *Tom Jones*.

There it serves a purpose so fundamental that it can come to seem as massive as the style of Gibbon, who seems to have realized this in his sentence of praise. He had already, in Chapter xxxii of the *Decline and Fall,* describing a Byzantine palace intrigue, compared it in a footnote to a passage of *Tom Jones,* "the romance of a great master, which may be considered the history of human nature." This would be about 1780; in 1789, discussing ancestors at the beginning of his *Autobiography,* for example the claim of Fielding's family to be related to the Hapsburgs, he said, "But the romance of *Tom Jones,* that exquisite picture of human manners, will outlive the palace of the Escurial and the imperial eagle of the House of Austria." This has more to do with Fielding than one might think, especially with his repeated claim, admitted to be rather comic but a major source of his nerve, that he was capable of making a broad survey because he was an aristocrat and had known high life from within. I take it that Gibbon meant his own irony not merely to attack the Christians (in that use it is "single") but to rise to a grand survey of the strangeness of human affairs. Of course both use it for protection against rival moralists, but its major use is to express the balance of their judgment. Fielding is already doing this in *Joseph Andrews,* but there the process seems genuinely casual. In *Tom Jones* he is expressing a theory about ethics, and the ironies are made to interlock with the progress of the demonstration. The titanic plot, which has been praised or found tiresome taken alone, was devised to illustrate the theory, and the screws of the engine of his style are engaging the sea. That is, the feeling that he is proving a case is what gives *Tom Jones* its radiance, making it immensely better, I think, than the other two novels (though perhaps there is merely less discovery about proving the sad truths of *Amelia*); it builds up like Euclid. Modern critics seem unable to feel this, apparently because it is forbidden by their aesthetic principles, even when Fielding tells them he is doing it; whereas Dr. Johnson and Sir John Hawkins, for example, took it seriously at once, and complained bitterly that the book had an immoral purpose. It certainly becomes much more interesting if you attend to its thesis; even if the thesis retains the shimmering mystery of a mirage.

Consider for example what Fielding says (XII.8) when he is reflecting over what happened when Sophia caught Tom in bed with Mrs. Waters at the Upton Inn, and incidentally telling us that that wasn't the decisive reason why Sophia rode away in anger, never likely to meet him again:

> I am not obliged to reconcile every matter to the received notions concerning truth and nature. But if this was never so easy to do, perhaps it might be more prudent in me to avoid it. For instance, as the fact before us now stands, without any comment of mine upon it, though it may at first sight offend some readers, yet, upon more mature consideration, it must please all; for wise and good men may consider what happened to Jones at Upton

as a just punishment for his wickedness in regard to women, of which it was indeed the immediate consequence; and silly and bad persons may comfort themselves in their vices by flattering their own hearts that the characters of men are owing rather to accident than to virtue. Now, perhaps the reflections which we should be here inclined to draw would alike contradict both these conclusions, and would show that these incidents contribute only to confirm the great, useful, and uncommon doctrine which it is the whole purpose of this work to inculcate, and which we must not fill up our pages by frequently repeating, as an ordinary parson fills up his sermon by repeating his text at the end of every paragraph.

He does, as I understand, partly tell us the doctrine elsewhere, but never defines it as his central thesis; perhaps he chooses to put the claim here because XII is a rather desultory book, fitting in various incidents which the plot or the thesis will require later, and conveying the slowness of travel before the rush of London begins in XIII. To say "the fact before us" makes Fielding the judge, and his readers the jury. He rather frequently warns them that they may not be able to understand him, and I think this leaves the modern critic, who assumes he meant nothing, looking rather comical. Perhaps this critic would say it is Empson who fails to see the joke of Fielding's self-deprecating irony; I answer that the irony of the book is double, here as elsewhere. Fielding realizes that any man who puts forward a general ethical theory implies a claim to have very wide ethical experience, therefore should be ready to laugh at his own pretensions; but also he isn't likely to mean nothing when he jeers at you for failing to see his point. Actually, the modern critic does know what kind of thing the secret is; but he has been badgered by neo-classicism and neo-Christianity and what not, whereas the secret is humanist, liberal, materialist, recommending happiness on earth and so forth; so he assumes it is dull, or the worldly advice of a flippant libertine.

Nobody would want to argue such points who had felt the tone of the book; it is glowing with the noble beauty of its gospel, which Fielding indeed would be prepared to claim as the original Gospel. The prose of generalized moral argument may strike us as formal, but it was also used by Shelley, who would also appeal to the Gospels to defend a moral novelty, as would Blake; an idea that the Romantics were original there seems to confuse people nowadays very much. When Fielding goes really high in *Tom Jones* his prose is like an archangel brooding over mankind, and I suppose is actually imitating similar effects in Handel; one might think it was like Bach, and that Handel would be too earthbound, but we know Fielding admired Handel. I admit that the effect is sometimes forced, and strikes us as the theatrical rhetoric of the Age of Sentiment; but you do not assume he is insincere there if you recognize that at other times the effect is very real.

A moderate case of this high language comes early in the book when Squire Allworthy is discussing charity with Captain Blifil (II.5). The captain is trying to ruin young Tom so as to get all the estate for himself, and has just remarked that Christian charity is an ideal, so ought not to be held to mean giving anything material; Allworthy falls into a glow at this, and readily agrees that there can be no merit in merely discharging a duty, especially such a pleasant one; but goes on:

> To confess the truth, there is one degree of generosity (of charity I would have called it), which seems to have some show of merit, and that is where, from a principle of benevolence and Christian love, we bestow on another what we really want ourselves; where, in order to lessen the distresses of another, we condescend to share some part of them, by giving what even our necessities cannot well spare. This is, I think, meritorious; but to relieve our brethren only with our superfluities—

—to do one thing and another, go the balanced clauses, "this seems to be only being rational creatures." Another theme then crosses his mind for the same grand treatment:

> As to the apprehension of bestowing bounty on such as may hereafter prove unworthy objects, merely because many have proved such, surely it can never deter a good man from generosity.

This too is argued with noble rhetoric, and then the captain inserts his poisoned barb. Now, the passage cannot be single irony, meant to show Allworthy as a pompous fool; he is viewed with wonder as a kind of saint (e.g. he is twice said to smile like an angel, and he is introduced as the most glorious creature under the sun), also he stood for the real benefactor Allen whom Fielding would be ashamed to laugh at. Fielding shows a Proust-like delicacy in regularly marking a reservation about Allworthy without ever letting us laugh at him (whereas critics usually complain he is an all-white character). Allworthy is something less than all-wise; the plot itself requires him to believe the villains and throw Tom out of Paradise Hall, and the plot is designed to carry larger meanings. The reason why he agrees so eagerly with the captain here, I take it, apart from his evidently not having experienced what he is talking about, is a point of spiritual delicacy or gentlemanly politeness—he cannot appear to claim credit for looking after his own cottagers, in talking to a guest who is poor; that was hardly more than looking after his own property, and the reflection distracts him from gauging the captain's motives. What is more important, he speaks as usual of doing good on principle, and here the central mystery is being touched upon.

One might think the answer is: "Good actions come only from good impulses, that is, those of a good heart, not from good principles"; the two bad tutors of Jones make this idea obvious at the beginning (especially III.5). Dr. Johnson and Sir John Hawkins denounced the book as meaning this, and hence implying that morality is no use (by the way, in my *Complex Words*, p. 173, I ascribed a sentence of Hawkins to Johnson, but they make the same points). Fielding might well protest that he deserved to escape this reproach; he had twice stepped out of his frame in the novel to explain that he was not recommending Tom's imprudence, and that he did not mean to imply that religion and philosophy are bad because bad men can interpret them wrongly. But he seems to have started from this idea in his first revolt against the ethos of Richardson which made him write *Shamela* and *Joseph Andrews*; I think it was mixed with a class belief, that well-brought-up persons (with the natural ease of gentlemen) do not need to keep prying into their own motives as these hypocritical Nonconformist types do. As a novelist he never actually asserts this idea, which one can see is open to misuse, and in *Tom Jones* (1749) he has made it only part of a more interesting idea; but, after he had been attacked for using it there, he arranged an ingenious reply in the self-defensive *Amelia* (1751). He gave the opinion outright to the silly Booth, a freethinker who disbelieves in free will (III.5); you are rather encouraged to regard Booth as a confession of the errors of the author when young. When he is converted at the end of the novel (XII.5) the good parson laughs at him for having thought this a heresy, saying it is why Christianity provides the motives of heaven and hell. This was all right as an escape into the recesses of theology; but it was the Calvinists who had really given up free will, and Fielding could hardly want to agree with them; at any rate Parson Adams, in *Joseph Andrews*, had passionately disapproved of salvation by faith. Fielding was a rather special kind of Christian, but evidently sincere in protesting that he was one. Adams is now usually regarded as sweetly Anglican, but his brother parson (in I.17) suspects he is the devil, after he has sternly rejected a series of such doctrines as give a magical importance to the clergy. I take it Fielding set himself up as a moral theorist, later than *Joseph Andrews*, because he decided he could refute the view of Hobbes, and of various thinkers prominent at the time who derived from Hobbes, that incessant egotism is logically inevitable or a condition of our being. We lack the moral treatise in the form of answers to Bolingbroke which he set out to write when dying, but can gather an answer from *Tom Jones*, perhaps from the firm treatment of the reader in VI.1, which introduces the troubles of the lovers and tells him that no author can tell him what love means unless he is capable of experiencing it. The doctrine is thus: "If good by nature, you can imagine other people's feelings so directly that you have an impulse to act on them as if they were your own; and this is the source of your greatest pleasures as well as of your only genuinely unselfish actions." A modern philosopher might answer that this makes no logical difference, but it clearly brings a large practical difference into the suasive effect of the argument of Hobbes, which was what people had thought worth discussing in the first place. The most striking illustration is in the sexual behavior of Jones, where he is most scandalous; one might, instead, find him holy, because he never makes love to a woman unless she first makes love to him. Later on (XIII.7) we find he thinks it a point of honor to accept such a challenge from a woman, no less than a challenge to fight from a man (and that is the absolute of honor, the duel itself); but in his first two cases, Molly Seagrim and Sophia, he is unconscious that their advances have aroused him, and very grateful when they respond. Fielding reveres the moral beauty of this, but is quite hardheaded enough to see that such a man is too easily fooled by women; he regards Tom as dreadfully in need of good luck, and feels like a family lawyer when he makes the plot give it to him. He is thus entirely sincere in repeating that Tom needed to learn prudence; but how this relates to the chastity enjoined by religion he does not explain. We may however observe that nobody in the novel takes this prohibition quite seriously all the time; even Allworthy, when he is friends again, speaks only of the imprudence of Tom's relations with Lady Bellaston (XVIII.10). In any case, the sexual affairs are only one of the many applications of the doctrine about mutuality of impulse; I think this was evidently the secret message which Fielding boasts of in *Tom Jones,* a book which at the time was believed to be so wicked that it had caused earthquakes.

We need not suppose he was well up in the long history of the question, but I would like to know more about his relations to Calvin; Professor C. S. Lewis, in his *Survey of Sixteenth-Century Literature,* brings out what unexpected connections Calvin can have. He maintained that no action could deserve heaven which was done in order to get to heaven; hence we can only attain good, that is non-egotist, motives by the sheer grace of God. In its early years the doctrine was by no means always regarded as grim; and it has an eerie likeness to the basic position of Fielding, that the well born soul has good impulses of its own accord, which only need directing. At least, a humble adherent of either doctrine may feel baffled to know how to get into the condition recommended. However, I take it this likeness arises merely because both men had seriously puzzled their heads over the Gospel, and tried to give its paradoxes their full weight. Fielding never made a stronger direct copy of a gospel parable than in *Joseph Andrews,* when Joseph is dying naked in the snow and an entire coachload finds worldly reasons for letting him die except for the postboy freezing on the outside, who gives Joseph his overcoat and is soon after transported for robbing a henroost. But I think he felt the paradoxes of Jesus more as a direct challenge after he had trained and practiced as a lawyer, and had come into line for a job as magistrate; that is, when he decided to write *Tom Jones.* He first wrote in favor of the Government on the 1745 Rebellion, in a stream of indignant pamphlets, and this was what made him possible as a magistrate; he was horrified at the public indifference at the prospect of a Catholic conquest, from which he expected rack and fire. He must then also be shocked at the indifference, or the moon-eyed preference for the invader, shown by all the characters in *Tom Jones*; nor can he approve the reaction of the Old Man of the Hill, who thanks God he has renounced so lunatic a world. To realize that Fielding himself is not indifferent here, I think, gives a further range to the vistas of the book, because all the characters are being as imprudent about it as Tom Jones about his own affairs; and this at least encourages one to suppose that there was a fair amount going on in Fielding's mind.

Tom Jones is a hero because he is born with good impulses; indeed, as the boy had no friend but the thieving gamekeeper Black George, among the lethal hatreds of Paradise Hall, he emerges as a kind of noble savage. This is first shown when, keen to shoot a bird, he follows it across the boundary and is caught on Squire Western's land; two guns were heard, but he insists he was alone. The keeper had yielded to his request and come too; if Tom says so, the keeper will be sacked, and his wife and children will starve, but Tom as a little gentleman at the great house can only be beaten. "Tom passed a very melancholy night" because he was afraid the beating might make him lose his honor by confessing, says Fielding, who adds that it was as severe as the tortures used in some foreign countries to induce confessions. The reader first learns to suspect the wisdom of Allworthy by hearing him say (III.2) that Tom acted here on a mistaken point of honor; though he only says it to defend Tom from further assaults by the bad tutors, who discuss the point with splendid absurdity. Whether it was "true," one would think, depended on whether the child thought Allworthy himself could be trusted not to behave unjustly. I have no respect for the critics who find the moralizing of the book too obvious; the child's honor really is all right after that; he is a fit judge of other ideas of honor elsewhere. Modern readers would perhaps like him better if they realized his basic likeness to Huck Finn; Mark Twain and Fielding were making much the same protest, even to the details about dueling. But Mark Twain somehow could not bear to have Huck grow up, whereas the chief idea about Tom Jones, though for various reasons it has not been recognized, is that he is planned to become awestrikingly better during his brief experience of the world. You are first meant to realize this is happening halfway through the book, when the Old Man of the Hill is recounting his life, and Tom is found smiling quietly to himself at a slight error in the ethical position of that mystical recluse (VIII.13). Old Man is a saint, and Fielding can provide him with some grand devotional prose, but he is too much of a stoic to be a real gospel Christian, which is what Tom is turning into as we watch him.

All critics call the recital of Old Man irrelevant, though Saintsbury labors to excuse it; but Fielding meant to give a survey of all human experience (that is what he meant by calling the book an epic) and Old Man provides the extremes of degradation and divine ecstasy which Tom has no time for; as part of the structure of ethical thought he is essential to the book, the keystone at the middle of the arch. The critics could not have missed understanding this if they hadn't imagined themselves forbidden to have intellectual interests, as Fielding had. For that matter, the whole setting of the book in the 1745 Rebellion gets its point when it interlocks with the theory and practice of Old Man. So far from being "episodic," the incident is meant to be such an obvious pulling together of the threads that it warns us to keep an eye on the subsequent moral development of Tom. As he approaches London unarmed, he is challenged by a highwayman; removing the man's pistol, and inquiring about the motives, he gives half of all he has to the starving family—rather more than half, to avoid calculation. Fielding of course knew very well that this was making him carry out one of the paradoxes of Jesus, though neither Fielding nor Tom must ever say so. The first time he earns money by selling his body to Lady Bellaston, a physically unpleasant duty which he enters upon believing at each step that his honor requires it (and without which, as the plot goes, he could probably not have won through to marrying Sophia), he tosses the whole fifty to his landlady, Mrs. Miller, for a hard luck case who turns out to be the same highwayman, though she will only take ten; when the man turns up to thank him, with mutual recognition, Tom congratulates him for having enough honor to fight for the lives of his children, and proceeds to Lady Bellaston "greatly exulting in the happiness he has procured," also reflecting on the evils that "strict justice" would have caused here (XIII.10). His next heroic action is to secure marriage for his landlady's daughter, pregnant by his fellow lodger Nightingale, thus "saving the whole family from destruction"; it required a certain moral depth, because the basic difficulty was to convince Nightingale that this marriage, which he greatly desired, was not forbidden to him by his honor. We tend now to feel that Tom makes a grossly obvious moral harangue, but Nightingale feels it has poohpoohed what he regards as the moral side of the matter, removing his "foolish scruples of honor" so that he can do what he prefers (XIV.7). Indeed the whole interest of the survey of ideas of honor is that different characters hold such different ones; no wonder critics who do not realize this find the repetition of the word tedious. These chapters in which the harangues of Tom are found obvious are interwoven with others in which his peculiar duty as regards Lady Bellaston has to be explained, and we pass on to the crimes which poor Lord Fellamar could be made to think his honor required. Critics would not grumble in the same way at Euclid, for being didactic in the propositions they have been taught already and immoral in the ones they refuse to learn. The threats of rape for Sophia and enslavement for Tom, as the plot works out, are simply further specimens of the code of honor; that danger for Tom is settled when Lord Fellamar gathers, still from hearsay, that the bastard is really a gentleman and therefore ought not to be treated as a kind of stray animal—he is "much concerned" at having been misled (XVIII.11). There is a less familiar point about codes of honor (indeed it struck the Tory critic Saintsbury as a libel on squires) when we find that Squire Western regards dueling as a Whig townee corruption, and proposes wrestling or singlestick with Lord Fellamar's second (XVI.2); but Fielding means Western to be right for once, not to prove that the old brute is a coward, and had said so in his picture of country life (V.12). When you consider what a tyrant Western is on his estate, it really does seem rather impressive that he carries no weapon.

Fielding meant all this as part of something much larger than a picture of the ruling-class code of honor; having taken into his head that he is a moral theorist, he has enough intelligence to be interested by the variety of moral codes in the society around him. A tribe, unlike a man, can exist by itself, and when found has always a code of honor (though not police, prisons and so forth) without which it could not have survived till found; such is the basis upon which any further moral ideas must be built. That is why Fielding makes Tom meet the King of the Gypsies, who can rule with no other force but shame because his people have no false honors among them (XII.12)—the incident is rather forced, because he is obviously not a gypsy but a Red Indian, just as Old Man, with his annuity and his housekeeper, has obviously no need to be dressed in skins like Robinson Crusoe; but they make you generalize the question. By contrast to this, the society which Fielding describes is one in which many different codes of honor, indeed almost different tribes, exist concurrently. The central governing class acts by only one of these codes and is too proud to look at the others (even Western's); but they would be better magistrates, and also happier and more sensible in their private lives, if they would recognize that these other codes surround them. It is to make this central point that Fielding needs the technique of double irony, without which one cannot express imaginative sympathy for two codes at once.

It strikes me that modern critics, whether as a result of the neo-Christian movement or not, have become oddly resistant to admitting that there is more than one code of morals in the world, whereas the central purpose of reading imaginative literature is to accustom yourself to this basic fact. I do not at all mean that a literary critic ought to avoid making moral judgments; that is useless as well as tiresome, because the reader has enough sense to start guessing round it at once. A critic had better say what his own opinions are, which can be done quite briefly, while recognizing that the person in view held different ones. (As for myself here, I agree with Fielding and wish I were as good.) The reason why Fielding could put a relativistic idea across on his first readers (though apparently not on modern critics) was that to them the word *honor* chiefly suggested the problem whether a gentleman had to duel whenever he was huffed; one can presume they were already bothered by it, because it was stopped a generation or two later—in England, though not in the America of Huckleberry Finn. But Fielding used this, as he used the Nightingale marriage, merely as firm ground from which he could be allowed to generalize; and he does not find relativism alarming, because he feels that to understand codes other than your own is likely to make your judgments better. Surely a "plot" of this magnitude is bound to seem tiresome unless it is frankly used as a means by which, while machining the happy ending, the author can present all sides of the question under consideration and show that his attitude to it is consistent. The professional Victorian novelists understood very well that Fielding had set a grand example there, and Dickens sometimes came near it, but it is a hard thing to plan for.

All the actions of Tom Jones are reported to Allworthy and Sophia, and that is why they reinstate him; they are his judges, like the reader. Some readers at the time said it was willful nastiness of Fielding to make Tom a bastard, instead of discovering a secret marriage at the end; and indeed he does not explain (XVIII.7) why Tom's mother indignantly refused to marry his father when her brother suggested it (Fielding probably knew a reason, liking to leave us problems which we can answer if we try, as Dr. Dudden's book shows, but I cannot guess it). But there is a moral point in leaving him a bastard; he is to inherit Paradise Hall because he is held to deserve it, not because the plot has been dragged round to make him the legal heir. Lady Mary Wortley Montagu, a grand second cousin of Fielding who thought him low, said that *Amelia* seemed to her just as immoral as his previous books, and she could not understand why Dr. Johnson forgave it, because it too encouraged young people to marry for love and expect a happy ending. She had enjoyed the books, and thought that Richardson's were just as immoral. I take it that, after a rather uncomfortable marriage for money, she found herself expected to give a lot of it away to her poor relations, so she thought they all ought to have married for money. Wrong though she may have been, the 18th century assumption that a novel has a moral seems to me sensible; *Tom Jones* really was likely to make young people marry for love, not only because that is presented as almost a point of honor but because the plot does not make the gamble seem hopeless. The machinery of the happy ending derives from the fairy tale, as Fielding perhaps recognized, as well as wanting to sound like Bunyan, when he called the house Paradise Hall. The third son seeking his fortune gives his crust to the withered crone and thus becomes a prince because she is Queen of the Fairies; the moral is that this was the right thing to do, even if she hadn't been, but the tale also suggests to the child that maybe this isn't such a bad bet as you might think, either. The mind of Fielding, as he gets near in the actual writing to the end of a plot which he is clearly following from a complete dated skeleton, begins to play round what it means when an author, as it were, tosses up to see whether to give his characters joy or sorrow; he is the creator here, he remarks, but he will promise not to work miracles, and so forth. Rather earlier, he positively asserts that generous behavior like Tom's is not rewarded with happiness on earth, indeed that it would probably be unchristian to suppose so. This is in one of the introductory chapters of literary prattle (XV.1); it is answered in XV.8, after a joke about whether Tom has selfish motives for a good action (and the reader who remembers IV.11 may well brace himself to hear a new scandal about Tom), by a firm assertion that the immediate results of such behavior are among the greatest happinesses that earth can provide. However, this play of mind does not arrive at telling us what the happy ending means, and indeed could not, as its chief function is to make the suspense real even for a thoughtful reader. I take it that the childish magic of the fairy tale, and its elder brother, the belief that good actions ought to be done because they will be rewarded in heaven, are reinforced in this novel by a practical idea which would not always apply; the outstanding moral of *Tom Jones*, if you look at it as Lady Mary did but less sourly, is that when a young man leaves home he is much more in a goldfish bowl than he thinks. The reader is to be influenced in favor of Tom's behavior by seeing it through the eyes of Allworthy and Sophia, whom one might think sufficiently high-class and severe. But the end conveys something much more impressive than that these examiners give him a pass degree; he has become so much of a gospel Christian that he cannot help but cast a shadow even on them. Against all reason and principle, and therefore to the consternation of Allworthy, he forgives Black George.

George robbed him, just after he was cast out, of the money Allworthy had given him to save him from degradation, for example, being pressed to sea as a vagabond, which nearly occurred. The gamekeeper was an old friend rather than a remote peasant, had become comfortable solely through the efforts of Tom to get him a job, and one would also think, as Tom's supposed natural-father-in-law, must have had an interest in letting him even now have a sporting chance. Fielding rated friendship specially highly, and always speaks of this betrayal in the tone of sad wonder he keeps for desperate cases. He says nothing himself about Tom forgiving George, but makes Allworthy give a harangue calling it wicked because harmful to society. We are accustomed in Fielding to hear

characters wriggle out of the absolute command by Jesus to forgive,
comically bad ones as a rule, and now the ideal landlord is saddled with
it. The time must clearly come, if a man carries through a consistent
program about double irony, when he himself does not know the answer;
and here, as it should do, it comes at the end of the novel. The practical
lawyer and prospective magistrate would have to find the Gospel puzzling
on this point; it is quite fair for Fielding still to refuse to admit that
Allworthy is in the wrong, because he may well suspect that the command of Jesus would bring anarchy. To be sure, this is not one of the
impressive tests of Tom; he is merely behaving nicely, just when everything is falling into his hands, and would lose our sympathy if he didn't;
it comes to him naturally, which not all the previous cases did. But still,
we have been moving through a landscape of the ethic of human
impulses, and when Tom rises above Allworthy he is like a mountain.

There is already a mystery or weird pathos about George when he is
first worked back into the plot (XV.12). Partridge is overjoyed, after all
their troubles in London, to meet someone who loves Tom so much:

> Betray you indeed! why I question whether you have a better friend than
> George upon earth, except myself, or one that would go further to serve
> you.

The reader is bound to take this as single irony at first, but Fielding is
soon cheerfully explaining that George really did wish Tom well, as
much as a man could who loved money more than anything else; and
then we get him offering money to Tom in prison. Though not allowed
to be decisive for the plot, he is useful in smuggling a letter to Sophia
and trustworthy in hiding it from his employer. As to his love of money,
we should remember that we have seen his family starving (III.9) after a
bad bit of 18th century administration by Allworthy. I think Fielding
means to play a trick, just after the theft, when he claims to put us fully
inside the mind of George; acting as go-between, George wonders whether
to steal also the bit of money sent by Sophia to the exile, and decides
that would be unsafe (VI.13). No doubt we are to believe the details,
but Fielding still feels free, in his Proust-like way, to give a different
picture of the man's character at the other end of the novel; I take it
he refused to believe that the "inside" of a person's mind (as given by
Richardson in a letter, perhaps) is much use for telling you the real
source of his motives. George of course has not reformed at the end; he
has arranged to come to London with his new employer, Western, the
more safely to cash the bill he stole, though, as he chooses the lawyer
who is the father of Nightingale, the precaution happens to be fatal. I
think the mind of Fielding held in reserve a partial justification for
George, though he was careful with it and would only express it in the

introductory prattle to Book XII, where both the case of George and its country setting are particularly far from our minds; indeed, I had to read the book again to find where this comment is put. While pretending to discuss literary plagiarism, Fielding lets drop that the villagers on these great estates consider it neither sin nor shame to rob their great neighbors, and a point of honor to protect any other villagers who have done so. George might assume, one can well imagine, that Tom was going to remain a grandee somehow whatever quarrels he had; in fact, Tom at the time is so much wrapped up in his unhappy love affair that he seems hardly to realize himself how much he will need money. On this view, it would be shameful for George to miss a chance of robbing Tom; for one thing, it would be robbing his own family, as the soldier reflects in VII.14. I agree that, so far from advancing this argument, Fielding never weakens the tone of moral shock with which he regards the behavior of George (who was right to be so ashamed that he ran away); but I think he means you to gather that the confusion between different moral codes made it intelligible. This background I think adds to the rather thrilling coolness with which Tom does not reply to the harangue of Allworthy denouncing his forgiveness; it is in any case time for him to go and dress to meet Sophia.

Sophia has the same kind of briefing as a modern Appointments Board; thus she does not waste time over his offer of marriage to Lady Bellaston; Sophia holds the document, but understands that this was merely the way to get rid of Lady Bellaston; so it joins the list of points already cleared. The decisive question in her mind is whether he has become a libertine, that is, whether his impulses have become corrupted; if they have, she is quite prepared again to refuse to unite by marriage the two largest estates in Somersetshire. Fielding has been blamed for making the forgiveness of Tom too easy, but I think his training as a bad playwright served him well here, by teaching him what he could throw away. A reader does not need to hear the case again, and Fielding disapproved of women who argue, indeed makes Allworthy praise Sophia for never doing it; and he himself has a certain shyness about expressing his doctrine, or perhaps thought it dangerous to express clearly. Beastly old Western comes yelling in to say for the average reader that we can't be bothered with further discussion of the matter, and Sophia decides that she can allow it to have settled itself. The fit reader, interested in the doctrine, is perhaps meant to feel rather disappointed that it is not preached, but also that this is good taste in a way, because after all the man's impulses have evidently not been corrupted. Even so, it is nothing like the view of Flaubert, Conrad and so forth, that a novelist is positively not allowed to discuss the point of his novel.

I want now, though there is so much else to choose from in this rich book, to say something about the thought of incest which terrifies Jones

in prison; both because it affects the judgment of Sophia and because
it has been a major bone of contention among other critics. Dr. F. H.
Dudden, in his treatise *Henry Fielding* (1952), though concerned to do
justice to an author whose morals have been maligned, admits that he
had a rather nasty habit of dragging fear of incest into his plots (it also
comes into *Joseph Andrews*); but decides that he means no harm by it,
and that it was probably just an effect of having to write bad plays when
he was young. On the other hand a *Times Lit. Supp.* reviewer, quoted
with indignation by Middleton Murry in *Unprofessional Essays,* had
thought this frightening of Jones a specially moral part of the plot. When
he goes to bed with Mrs. Waters at Upton, says the reviewer, Fielding

> seems to be making light of it, or even conniving at it. Yet it is the first step
> in a moral progress downhill. . . . And then, much later in the book, evi-
> dence comes to light which suggests [that she was his mother]. . . . Field-
> ing's connivance was a pretence. He has sprung a trap on Tom and us; he
> has made us realize—as a serious novelist always makes us realize, and a
> frivolous novelist often makes us forget—that actions have their conse-
> quences. . . . It is this sense of the moral structure of life that makes Field-
> ing important.

I could have quoted more sanctimonious bits, but this was the part
which Middleton Murry found perverse:

> What to a more normal sensibility constitutes the one doubtful moment in
> the book—the one moment at which we feel that Fielding *may* have
> sounded a wrong note, by suggesting an awful possibility outside the range
> of the experience he invites us to partake—becomes in this vision the one
> thing which makes the book considerable.

The reviewer of course was trying to speak up for Fielding, and make
him something better than a flippant libertine; and it is in favor of his
view that the Upton incident is the one place where Fielding says in
person that casual sex is forbidden by Christianity as expressly as murder
(IX.3). Dr. Dudden might be expected to agree with the reviewer; he
maintains you have only to attend to the text to find that Fielding always
not only denounces sin but arranges to have it punished "inexorably and
terribly." This indeed is one half of what Fielding intended, though the
adverbs hardly describe the purring tone of the eventual forgiveness of
Tom, as when we are told that he has, "by reflection on his past follies,
acquired a discretion and prudence very uncommon in one of his lively
parts." Instead, we find that Dr. Dudden agrees with Middleton Murry;
they are more in sympathy with Fielding than the reviewer, but feel they
have to confess that the incest trick is rather bad; chiefly, I think, because
they like him for being healthy, and that seems clearly not.
I think the basic reason why Fielding twice uses this fear is that he had

a philosophical cast of mind, and found it curious that those who laugh
at ordinary illicit sex take incest very seriously. As to *Joseph Andrews,*
the starting point is that Fielding is to parody Richardson's Pamela,
a servant who made her master marry her by refusing to be seduced. He
had already done this briefly and fiercely in *Shamela,* where an ex-prosti-
tute acts like Pamela out of conscious calculation—the moral is that
Pamela is *unconsciously* calculating, and that girls ought not to be
encouraged to imitate this minx. He is now to do it by swapping the
sexes; a footman would be cowardly, or have some other low motive,
if he refused a lady, and a lady would be lacking in the delicacy of her
caste if she even wanted a footman. Thus the snobbish Fielding, in
opposition to the democratic Richardson, can prove that the class
structure ought not to be disturbed. Or rather, he did not actually have
to write this stuff, because he could rely on his readers to imagine he had,
as they still do. It is false to say, as is regularly said, that Fielding started
on his parody and then wrote something else because he found he was
a novelist; he did not start on it at all. From the first words, he treats
his story with an almost overrefined, a breathless delicacy; and by the
time Lady Booby has offered marriage, and Joseph, though attracted
by her, still refuses her because he wants to marry his humble sweetheart,
most of the laughing readers should be pretty well outfaced. No doubt
Fielding himself, if the story had been outlined at his club, would have
laughed as heartily as the others; but he is concerned in this novel, where
he is rather oddly safe from being thought a hypocrite, to show that his
sympathy is so broad that he can see the question all round, like a judge.
I think he did discover something in writing it, but not what is usually
said; he discovered how much work he could leave the public to do for
him. One type of reader would be jeering at Joseph, and another admiring him, and feeling indignant with the first type; and both of them
would hardly notice what the author was writing down. You can understand that he might want to take some rather firm step, towards the end,
to recover their attention. What he is really describing is the chastity of
the innocent Joseph, adding of course the piercing simplicity of his
criticisms of the great world; Parson Adams, whom Fielding certainly
does not intend us to think contemptible, preaches to him a rather over-
strained doctrine of chastity all along. Just as all seems ready for the
happy ending with his humble sweetheart, a twist of the plot makes them
apparently brother and sister; they decide to live together chastely, as
Parson Adams had always said they should be able to do. Here the club-
men who form Type A of the intended readers no longer dare to jeer at
Joseph for believing he has a duty of chastity; the opposed groups are
forced to combine. I thus think that this turn of the plot is entirely
justified; for that matter, I think that modern critics are rather too fond
of the strategic device of claiming to be embarrassed.

In *Tom Jones*, I can't deny, the trick is chiefly used to heighten the excitement at the end of the plot—Tom must go either right up or right down. I agree with the *Times Lit. Supp.* reviewer that it marks a change in the attitude of hero, but it comes only as an extra at the end of a gradual development. Saintsbury defended Tom's relations with Lady Bellaston by saying that the rule against a gentleman taking money from a mistress had not yet been formulated; certainly it doesn't seem to have hampered the first Duke of Marlborough, but Tom comes to suspect of his own accord that some such rule has been formulated. He felt it when he first met Sophia in London (XIII.11); "the ignominious circumstance of his having been kept" rose in his mind when she began to scold him, and stopped his mouth; the effect of this was good, because her actual accusations came as a relief and were the more easy to argue off convincingly. It is not till XV.9 that Nightingale, as a fair return for the teaching of basic morals, warns him that he is liable to become despised by the world, and explains that the way to break with Lady Bellaston is to offer her marriage. Learning that he is one of a series makes Tom feel free to break with her, which he thought before would be ungrateful. By the way, I take it Fielding admired her firmness about marriage, as a protest against unjust laws on women's property; her criminal plot against the lovers is chiefly meant as a satire against the worldly code—she can be taken as sincere in telling Lord Fellamar that the intention is to save her ward Sophia from ruin, and Fielding only means to describe her unconsciousness when he adds in XVI.8 that women support this code out of jealousy. Tom refuses to marry a rich widow immediately afterwards (XV.11); this is the sternest of his tests, and he is "put into a violent flutter," because he suspects it is a duty of honor to accept this fortune so as to release Sophia from misery. He seems like Galahad when he rejects the point of honor for love, and it does prove that in learning "prudence," which is how Fielding and Allworthy describe his moral reform, he is not falling into the opposite error of becoming a calculating type. We next have him refusing to make love to Mrs. FitzPatrick, while easily rejecting her spiteful advice to make love to Sophia's aunt (XVI.9). Both she and Lady Bellaston are affronted by his frank preference for Sophia and yet find their passions excited by its generosity—"strange as it may seem, I have seen many instances." The last of the series is his refusal to go to bed with Mrs. Waters when she visits him in jail with the news that her supposed husband is not dying, so that he is safe from execution (XVII.9); this might seem ungenerous rather than reformed, but he has just heard from Mrs. Miller that Sophia has become determined to refuse him because of his incontinency. The next and final book opens with the supposed discovery that Mrs. Waters is his mother, so that he committed incest with her at Upton. This throws him into a state of shaking horror which serves to illustrate his courage; we realize how undisturbed he was before at the prospect of being hanged for an act of self-defense. It is thus not the case that Tom was shocked into disapproving of his previous looseness by the thought that it might cause accidental incest, because this fear came after he had become prudent; still less that the fear of death and the horror of incest were needed together to crack such a hard nut as the conscience of Tom, because he has been freed from the fear of death just before the other alarm arrives. (I understand he was technically in danger under ecclesiastical law, but prosecution was very unlikely; in any case the question never occurs to him.) Fielding as a magistrate, surely, would think it contemptible to cheat a prisoner into reform by this trick, whereas the *Times Lit. Supp.* reviewer seems to assume it would be moral. What one can say is that the shock puts Tom into a grave frame of mind, suitable for meeting Sophia; and Sophia really does need winning over, with some extra moral solemnity however acquired, because she is quite pigheaded enough to fly in the face of the world all over again, and start refusing Tom just because he has become the heir.

My own objection to this bit about incest has long been something quite different, which I should think occurs oftener to a modern reader; and I think the book feels much better when it is cleared up. I thought the author was cheating in a way that whodunit authors often do, that is, he put in a twist to make the end more exciting though the characters would not really have acted so. Those who dislike Fielding generally say that he makes his characters so obvious, especially from making them so selfish, that they become tiresome like performing toys; but the reason why Mrs. Waters gets misunderstood here is that here as always she is unusually generous-minded. A penniless but clever girl, she learned Latin under Partridge when he was a village schoolmaster and did so well that he kept her on as an assistant, but she learned too much Latin; a fatal day came (II.3) when he jovially used Latin to ask her to pass a dish at dinner, and "the poor girl smiled, perhaps at the badness of the Latin, and, when her mistress cast eyes upon her, blushed, possibly with a consciousness of having laughed at her master." This at once made Mrs. Partridge certain not only that they were lovers but that they were jeering at her by using this code in her presence; and such is the way most of us fail to understand her final letter. A ruinous amount of fuss goes on, and it becomes convenient for her to work with Allworthy's sister in the secret birth of Jones, acting as her personal servant at the great house and paid extra to take the scandal of being his mother before leaving the district. The story is improbable, but as Fielding arranges it you can call it credible. Allworthy gives her a grand sermon against illicit love when she confesses to the bastard, but is impressed by the honor and generosity of her replies; he sends her an allowance, but stops it when he hears she has run off with a sergeant. We next see her when

Jones saves her life (IX.2); the villain Northerton is trying to murder her for what money she carries, and it is startling for the reader to be told, what Jones is too delicate to ask her (IX.7), that she was only wandering about with this man to save him from being hanged, and only carrying the money to give it to him. She had expected to rejoin Captain Waters after his winter campaign against the rebels, but meanwhile Lieutenant Northerton was afraid of being hanged for murdering Jones (whereas it had been very lucky for Jones that the drunken assault removed him from the army), and needed to be led across hill country to a Welsh port. Fielding always admires women who can walk, instead of being tight-laced and townee, and though he tends to grumble at learned women he had evidently met a variety of them; he can forgive Mrs. Waters her Latin. She need not be more than thirty-six when she meets Tom, and the struggle has exposed her breasts, which it appears have lasted better than her face. She stops Tom from hunting for Northerton,

> earnestly entreating that he would accompany her to the town whither they had been directed. "As to the fellow's escape," said she, "it gives me no uneasiness; for philosophy and Christianity both preach up forgiveness of injuries. But for you, sir, I am concerned at the trouble I give you; nay, indeed, my nakedness may well make you ashamed to look me in the face; and if it were not for the sake of your protection, I would wish to go alone."
>
> Jones offered her his coat; but, I know not for what reason, she absolutely refused the most earnest solicitation to accept it. He then begged her to forget both the causes of her confusion.

He walks before her all the way so as not to see her breasts, but she frequently asks him to turn and help her. The seduction is entirely free from any further designs on him; she is as foot-loose as a character in the *Faerie Queene,* though perhaps her happening to fall in with FitzPatrick next morning at the Upton Inn is what saves Jones from finding her even a momentary responsibility. Even so, her capacity to handle Fitz-Patrick is rather impressive; the only occupation of this gentleman is to hunt for the woman he cheated into marriage in the hope of bullying her out of what little of her money is secured from him by the law, after wasting the rest; one would hardly think he was worth milking, let alone the unpleasantness of his company, so that she had better have gone back to her officer. Perhaps she wanted to get to London; the only story about her is that she is independent. We are told at the end that she eventually married Parson Supple.

When Fielding says he doesn't know the reason he always means it is too complicated to explain. Walking with her lifesaver Jones she liked to appear pathetic, and she wanted to show her breasts, but also she really could not bear to let him take his coat off, not on such a cold night. The decision becomes a nuisance when they get to the inn because it makes her almost unacceptable, but this is got over; and she gathers from the landlady that Jones is in love with a younger woman.

> The awkward behavior of Mr. Jones on this occasion convinced her of the truth, without his giving a direct answer to any of her questions; but she was not nice enough in her amours to be particularly concerned at the discovery. The beauty of Jones highly charmed her eye; but as she could not see his heart she gave herself no concern about it. She could feast heartily at the table of love, without reflecting that some other had been, or hereafter might be, feasted with the same repast. A sentiment which, if it deals but little in refinement, deals, however, much in substance; and is less capricious, and perhaps less ill-natured and selfish, than the desires of those females who can be contented enough to abstain from the possession of their lovers, provided that they are sufficiently satisfied that nobody else possesses them.

This seems to me a particularly massive bit of double irony, worthy to outlast the imperial eagles of the House of Austria, though I take it Fielding just believed what he said, and only knew at the back of his mind that the kind of man who would otherwise complain about it would presume it was irony.

Such is our main background information about Mrs. Waters when she visits him in prison, assures him that her supposed husband is recovering fast so that there is no question of murder, and is rather cross with him for refusing to make love to her. Then her entirely unexpected letter arrives, which I must give in full (XVIII.2):

> Sir—Since I left you I have seen a gentleman, from whom I have learned something concerning you which greatly surprises and affects me; but as I have not at present leisure to communicate a matter of such high importance, you must suspend your curiosity till our next meeting, which shall be the first moment I am able to see you. Oh, Mr. Jones, little did I think, when I passed that happy day at Upton, the reflection upon which is like to embitter all my future life, who it was to whom I owed such perfect happiness.—Believe me to be ever sincerely your unfortunate
>
> J. Waters.
>
> P.S.—I would have you comfort yourself as much as possible, for Mr. Fitzpatrick is in no manner of danger; so that, whatever other grievous crimes you may have to repent of, the guilt of blood is not among the number.

Partridge, who happened not to see Mrs. Waters at Upton, has seen her visit the prison and eavesdropped on her talk with Jones; so he has just horrified Jones by telling him she is his mother; they think this letter confirms the belief, and certainly it is hard to invent any other meaning. We are not told who the gentleman was till XVIII.8, when she tells Allworthy that the lawyer Dowling had visited her, and told her that

> if Mr. Jones had murdered my husband, I should be assisted with any money I wanted to carry on the prosecution, by a very worthy gentleman,

who, he said, was well apprised what a villain I had to deal with. It was by this man I discovered who Mr. Jones was. . . . I discovered his name by a very odd accident; for he himself refused to tell it to me; but Partridge, who met him at my lodgings the second time he came, knew him formerly at Salisbury.

She assumed it was Allworthy who was persecuting Jones in this relentless manner, whereas Allworthy knows it must be Blifil, whom Dowling hopes to blackmail; and since she greatly revered Allworthy, though herself some kind of freethinker, she assumed that Jones had done something to deserve it—this explains the postscript "whatever other grievous crimes." "The second time" is an important detail; the second time Dowling came must have been after she wrote the letter, and was the first time Partridge came. As soon as Partridge saw her he would tell her Jones's fear of incest and she would dispel it; but Partridge has to come, to meet Dowling and tell her his name (otherwise the plot of Blifil could not be exposed). We have next to consider how she knew, when she wrote the letter, about the anger of Sophia; but Jones would tell her this himself, when she visited him in prison, because he would feel he had to offer a decent reason for refusing to go to bed with her. A deep generosity, when she has thought things over after the unpleasant talk with Dowling, is what makes her write down that if Sophia refuses to marry Tom it will embitter all the rest of her life. The delusion about incest is the kind of mistake which is always likely if you interpret in selfish terms the remarks of a very unselfish character. Certainly, the coincidences of the plot are rigged almost to the point where we reject them unless we take them as ordained by God; Fielding would be accustomed to hearing pious characters call any bit of luck a wonderful proof of providence, and might hope they would feel so about his plot— as Partridge encourages them to do (e.g. XII.8). But the reaction of the character to the plot is not rigged; she behaves as she always does.

I ought finally to say something about his attitude to the English class system, because opinions about what he meant there seem often to be decisive for the modern reader. What people found so entertaining at the time, when Fielding attacked Richardson in a rather explosive class situation (the eager readers of Richardson in French were presumably heading toward the French Revolution) was that the classes seemed to have swapped over. The printer's apprentice was the gentlemanly expert on manners, indeed the first English writer to be accepted as one by the polite French; whereas if you went to see Fielding, they liked to say at the time, you would find him drunk in bed with his cook and still boasting he was related to the Hapsburgs. His answer to Richardson was thus: "But I know what a gentleman is; I am one." The real difference was about the meaning of the term; Fielding thought it should mean a man fit to belong to the class which actually rules in his society, especially by being a just judge. His behavior eventually made a lot of people feel he had won the argument, though not till some time after his death. To die poor and despised while attempting to build up the obviously needed London Police Force, with obvious courage and humanity, creating astonishment by his refusal to accept the usual bribes for such dirty work, and leaving the job in hands which continued it—this became too hard to laugh off; he had done in the heart of London what empire-builders were being revered for doing far away. He provided a new idea of the aristocrat, with the added claim that it was an older tradition; and he did seem to clear the subject up rather—you could hardly deny that he was a better idea than Lord Chesterfield. An impression continued that, if you are very rude and rough, that may mean you are particularly aristocratic, and good in an emergency; I doubt whether, without Fielding, the Victorian novelists (however much they forbade their daughters to read his books) would have retained their trust in the rather hidden virtues of the aristocracy.

Much of this was wished onto Fielding later, but we have a series of jokes against the current idea of a gentleman during Tom's journey to London. The remarks in favor of the status are perhaps what need picking out. Tom leaves Old Man because he hears cries for help; he thus saves the life of Mrs. Waters from the villain Northerton, who might seem to justify the contempt for mankind of Old Man. This is at the beginning of Book IX; at the very end of it, after the reader has learned how bad the case is, Fielding urges him not to think he means to blame army officers in general:

> Thou wilt be pleased to consider that this fellow, as we have already informed thee, had neither the birth nor the education of a gentleman, nor was a proper person to be enrolled among the number of such. If, therefore, his baseness can justly reflect on any besides himself, it must be only on those who gave him his commission.

We learn incidentally, from this typical rounding on an administrator, that Fielding presumed men ought to be promoted to the ruling class, as a regular thing; the point is merely that the system of promotion should be adequate to save it from contempt. The exalted cynicism of Old Man (who by the way did not try to help Mrs. Waters, though he and not Tom had a gun) might make one suspect that adequate members of such a class cannot be found, and Fielding has kept in mind the social question of how you should do it. I have known readers think Fielding wanted to abolish gentlemen, and indeed the jokes against them are pretty fierce; but he had planted another remark at the beginning of Book IX, in the chapter of introductory prattle, which is clearly meant to fit the last words of that Book. An author needs to have experienced both low life and high life, he is saying; low life for honesty and sincerity; high life, dull and absurd though it is, for elegance, and a liberality of spirit; which last quality I have myself scarce ever seen in men of low birth and education.

The assertion seems moderate, perhaps hardly more than that most men don't feel free to look all round a question, unless their position is comfortable enough; but "liberality of spirit" feels rather near to the basic virtue of having good impulses. Of course, he does not mean that all gentlemen have it; the total egotism of young Blifil, a theoretically interesting case, with a breakdown into sadism, which critics have chosen to call unlifelike, is chiefly meant to make clear that they do not. But it seems mere fact that Fielding's society needed a governing class, however things may work out under universal education; so it is reasonable of him to take a reformist view, as the Communists would say, and merely recommend a better selection.

Indeed, it is perhaps flat to end this essay with an example which yields so placid a solution to a build-up of "double irony"; nor is it a prominent example, because after we get to London the ironies are about honor rather than gentility. But I suspect that today both halves of the puzzle about gentlemen are liable to work against him; he gets regarded as a coarse snob, whose jovial humor is intended to relax the laws only in favor of the privileged. This at least is unjust; no one attacked the injustices of privilege more fiercely. His position was not found placid at the time, and there is one class paradox which he repeatedly labored to drive home; though to judge from a survey of opinions on him (*Fielding the Novelist,* F. H. Blanchard, 1926) this line of defense never gave him any protection in his lifetime. "Only low people are afraid of having the low described to them, because only they are afraid of being exposed as themselves low." The paradox gives him a lot of powerful jokes, but so far from being farfetched it follows directly from his conception of a gentleman, which was if anything a literal-minded one. He means by it a person fit to sit on the bench as a magistrate, and naturally such a man needs to know all about the people he is to judge; indeed, the unusual thing about Fielding as a novelist is that he is always ready to consider what he would do if one of his characters came before him when he was on the bench. He is quite ready to hang a man, but also to reject the technical reasons for doing so if he decides that the man's impulses are not hopelessly corrupted. As to the reader of a novel, Fielding cannot be bothered with him unless he too is fit to sit on a magistrate's bench, prepared, in literature as in life, to handle and judge any situation. That is why the reader gets teased so frankly. The same kind of firmness, I think, is what makes the forgiveness by Tom at the end feel startling and yet sensible enough to be able to stand up to Allworthy. I think the chief reason why recent critics have belittled Fielding is that they find him intimidating.

Tom Jones: Life as Art

by Andrew Wright

"As I am in reality," Fielding writes at the beginning of Book II of *Tom Jones,* "the founder of a new province of writing, so I am at liberty to make what laws I please therein." In the corresponding chapter in *Joseph Andrews* ("Of divisions in authors"—II,1), Fielding's relationship to his readers is magisterial, masterful. But, as he demonstrates from the very beginning of *Tom Jones,* and far more explicitly than in the earlier novel, he intends to be Master of the Revels. The title of the first chapter of the first book of *Tom Jones* is "The introduction to the work, or bill of fare to the feast." On the image which Fielding produces just here, the meaning of the novel depends. He says here that an author ought to regard himself in the same light as the master of an ordinary who, in order to prevent any disappointment to his customers, brings before them a bill of fare, and they, "having thence acquainted themselves with the entertainment which they may expect, may either stay and regale with what is provided for them, or may depart to some other ordinary better accommodated to their taste." Fielding is asking us to take *Tom Jones* in this festive spirit.

The "provision" of the feast is human nature. He is going to use the facts of life—what others are there?—to make an artifact.[1] He deals with the possible objection "from the more delicate, that this dish is too common and vulgar," by insisting that "true nature is as difficult to be met with in authors as the Bayonne ham, or Bologna sausage, is to be found in the shops." Fielding knows that to be false to life is to be faithless to art. Correspondingly, when he tells the truth about life it is for the noble purpose of providing a feast. Indeed, the very structure of *Tom*

[1] Compare Wayne Booth: "Much as Fielding and Dickens, Trollope and Thackeray may talk about their passion for truth to nature or the real, they are often willing, as some modern critics have complained, to sacrifice reality to tears or laughter" (*The Rhetoric of Fiction,* p. 57).

Jones is put in terms of the dishes of the banquet which he is going to lay before us: "we shall represent human nature at first to the keen appetite of our reader, in that more plain and simple manner in which it is found in the country, and shall hereafter hash and ragoo it with all the high French and Italian seasoning of affectation and vice which courts and cities afford." [2]

My point in subtitling this book *Mask and Feast* is of course to yoke the two, I trust not by violence, together. Fielding puts on the mask of tavernkeeper and serves up to his readers the varied dishes of human nature. A mask is already a disguise, and a masquerade is itself an entertainment, beguiling because false. Or is it that a masquerade offers the truth of hyperbole? At all events, it is to this other controlling image that I now wish to turn. Fielding provides it for us, spaciously and even expansively, in the first chapter of Book VII. It is called, and is, "A comparison between the world and the stage."

The only partly concealed premise of this chapter is that bad art results from distortion of human motive, this in turn proceeding from poor observation; by the same token, good art is founded on an accurate apprehension of the nature of man. This is all usual enough. What is unusual in this chapter is the insistence on making the reader understand *Tom Jones* within a theatrical framework: Bad art can afford to look like life because it is false; good art, on the other hand, being based upon life, must be distanced by the mechanism of art. An art founded upon life must be artificial or it will be unbearable.

For after reminding the reader that the world and the stage have often been compared, Fielding offers as an alternative reason for the comparison the Aristotelian argument that "the theatrical stage is . . . an imitation of what really exists," and he rejects this alternative. The actors remain actors, "whom we use as children frequently do the instruments of their amusement; and have much more pleasure in hissing and buffeting them, than in admiring their excellence." So that Fielding is in effect drawing the line between life and art, as later did that other man of common sense, the Scotsman David Hume.

It may be possible to think that Fielding is adversely criticizing bad plays or poor audiences or both—or it would be possible to think so if he proceeded otherwise than he actually does, in his argument. He argues that the world and the stage may be compared because men themselves masquerade as what they are not; "thus the hypocrite may be said to be a player; and indeed the Greeks called them both by one and the same name." This is familiar Fielding territory, a favorite preoccupation because it is based upon an idea of character which lends itself to such

[2] Wilbur Cross, in *The History of Henry Fielding*, II, 104f, points out that this first chapter elaborates on a letter written by Fielding in *The True Patriot* for December 3, 1745.

reflection. Here, therefore, he would seem to be pointing to the artificiality with which much human motive is disguised.

Perhaps because there is nothing very original about what Fielding says here, the significance of his line of argument is not always noticed. For Fielding enters a plea the force of which is felt the more strongly if what precedes it has been taken into account. "In all these, however, and in every other similitude of life to the theatre, the resemblance hath been always taken from the stage only. None, as I remember, have at all considered the audience at this great drama." He thereupon proceeds to guess how *his* audience—from upper gallery to pit and boxes—will react to "that scene which Nature was pleased to exhibit in the twelfth chapter of the preceding book, where she introduced Black George running away with the £500 from his friend and benefactor."

Fielding in fact turns convention upside down by requiring us to think of the Black George flight as fictional. The History of Tom Jones is history in a very special sense. Morally it is true. But it is true because it is a fiction. The realism of technique designedly gives way to, indeed paves the way to, what becomes a masquerade. This is true because to see life spectacularly is to be generous about human motive. At a distance even Mrs. Tow-wouse and Parson Trulliber and Beau Didapper are endurable, and there is not much good to be said about such characters. Black George, however, belongs in a special category of which the definition does not become complete until *Tom Jones*.

> Now we, who are admitted behind the scenes of this great theatre of Nature (and no author ought to write anything besides dictionaries and spelling books who hath not this privilege), can censure the action, without conceiving any absolute detestation of the person whom perhaps Nature may not have designed to act an ill part in all her dramas; for in this instance life most exactly resembles the stage, since it is often the same person who represents the villain and the hero; and he who engages your admiration today will probably attract your contempt tomorrow.

In the context of his thinking about human nature, this remark of Fielding's is compelling. Most men, in Fielding's view, are positively evil from birth: such a person is Blifil; or at best wicked through indifference, selfishness, or ambition: such a person is Black George. Black George acts the bad part but is not evil—and Fielding dares us to be charitable to him. He goes further, because he dares us to be uncharitable. "The worst of men generally have the words rogue and villain most in their mouths, as the lowest of all wretches are the aptest to cry out low in the pit." This remark goes some of the distance toward a definition of Fielding's special brand of contempt for mankind. In a later chapter (X,1) he makes further remarks to the purpose. In this chapter, "Containing instructions very necessary to be perused by modern critics," Fielding gives a number of cautions to the reader, the most important of which is "not to condemn a character as a bad one because it is not perfectly a good one." And for Fielding the supreme generosity is to be charitable without the expectation of gratitude. Such is the "second self" he creates as master of the revels in *Tom Jones*.

A fine sample of Fielding's special domination over the novel which he constructs for our delight occurs in chapter seven of Book III, the chapter title of which is "In which the author himself makes his appearance on the stage." Here is a brace of paragraphs in which is contained, I think, the heart of the novel. At the beginning of the chapter Fielding explains that Mrs. Blifil's open preference for Tom, at the expense of young Blifil himself, was such as to make the fair and charitable Squire Allworthy compassionate toward Blifil, and at the same time think less well of Tom than he might otherwise have done, especially as Tom's own "wantonness, wildness, and want of caution" invited adverse judgment. Then comes the narrator's admonition

> to those well-disposed youths who shall hereafter be our readers; for they may here find that goodness of heart and openness of temper, though these may give them greater comfort within, and administer to an honest pride in their own minds, will by no means, alas! do their business in the world. Prudence and circumspection are necessary even to the best of men. . . . It is not enough that your designs, nay, that your actions are intrinsically good; you must take care they shall appear so. If your inside be never so beautiful, you must preserve a fair outside also. This must be constantly looked to, or malice and envy will take care to blacken it so, that the sagacity and goodness of an Allworthy will not be able to see through it, and to discern the beauties within. Let this, my young readers, be your constant maxim, that no man can be good enough to enable him to neglect the rules of prudence; nor will Virtue herself look beautiful unless she be bedecked with the outward ornaments of decency and decorum. And this precept, my worthy disciples, if you read with due attention, you will, I hope, find sufficiently enforced by examples in the following pages.

This long admonitory passage must not be taken at face value. Again and again, Fielding as narrator stands between his novel and a didactic interpretation of the course of the narrative, not least when he is pretending to be didactic. For as a preacher he always goes too far, protests too much, and thus invites more and less than a straightforward response. For after the paragraph from which I have just quoted, follows another which must, I think, be taken as qualification of what has preceded. "I ask pardon," Fielding writes,

> for this short appearance, by way of chorus, on the stage. It is in reality for my own sake that, while I am discovering the rocks on which innocence and goodness often split, I may not be misunderstood to recommend the very means to my worthy readers by which I intend to show them they

will be undone. And this, as I could not prevail on any of my actors to speak, I myself was obliged to declare.

The final sentence of that paragraph—it is also the last sentence of the chapter—gives conclusively away the festive intent of *Tom Jones*. Behind the smile of the narrator lies condonation of the hero. This, which Allworthy was incapable of—at least until the end of the novel—we are invited to share and to rejoice in, from very near the beginning.

In fact, the most substantial of the preliminary chapters in *Tom Jones* —the opening chapter of Book VIII—is devoted to an attack on verisimilitude. It is called "A wonderful long chapter concerning the marvelous; being much the longest of all our introductory chapters." In insisting on verisimilitude he manages to enlarge the boundaries to the very limits of human credibility.[3] The chapter is a pastiche of neoclassical arguments, looking not without nostalgia to the Homeric days when it was natural to introduce heathen deities, and characteristically at what can be the subject of art nowadays: "Man . . . is the highest subject (unless on very extraordinary occasions indeed) which presents itself to the pen of our historian, or of our poet; and, in relating his actions, great care is to be taken that we do not exceed the capacity of the agent we describe." After a series of reflections on the consequences of this necessary focus, Fielding concludes with a dictum which, partly because of its very unoriginality, will provide him with a warrant for the events within Book VIII itself.

> For though every good author will confine himself within the bounds of probability, it is by no means necessary that his characters, or his incidents, should be trite, common, or vulgar; such as happen in every street, or in every house, or which may be met with in the home articles of a newspaper. Nor must he be inhibited from showing many persons and things, which may possibly have never fallen within the knowledge of great part of his readers. If the writer strictly observes the rules above-mentioned, he hath discharged his part; and is then entitled to some faith from his reader, who is indeed guilty of critical infidelity if he disbelieves him.[4]

This is an invocation to belief made by an author who in the following pages will stretch as far as is possible his reader's capacity for maintaining faith. Book VIII is crowded with surprises, with jaunty ex-

---

[3] See Ian Watt on the neoclassical idea of requiring and reconciling both verisimilitude and the marvelous *(The Rise of the Novel*, pp. 252f.).

[4] Henry James writes approvingly of Fielding ("he handsomely possessed of a mind") as narrator of *Tom Jones*: "Fielding's fine old moralism, fine old humor and fine old style . . . somehow really enlarge, make every one and every thing important" (Preface to *The Princess Casamassima*, reprinted in *The Art of the Novel* [New York, 1934], p. 68).

periments in extravagance, with meticulous arrangement of plot. There is little Benjamin, a learned barber—who reveals himself not merely as Partridge but also as the man who is assuredly not Tom's father. Surely it is fair to say that the reader recognizes the action of this book to be contrived—and yet sees within or behind the contrivance adequacy of human motivation. Such is Fielding at his most characteristic: within an entirely artificial context, made up—paradoxically—of the most natural and realistic elements, appear characters who behave with a verisimilar consistency, or inconsistency. Thus in chapter 7 of this book, Partridge's reason for attaching himself to Tom is shown to be less than fully disinterested. "It came into his head, therefore, that if he could prevail with the young gentleman to return back to his father [as Partridge mistakenly thought Allworthy to be] he should by that means render a service to Allworthy which would obliterate all his former anger." Nor is the manner of the telling of his story by the Man of the Hill, which also occurs in this book, to be overlooked. Like the story of Wilson in *Joseph Andrews,* the Man of the Hill's tale is repeatedly interrupted. The interrupter here is Partridge, and his intervention prevents the moralizing from making of *Tom Jones* what Fielding does not believe in, a novel with a moral.

Fielding calls one of his prefatory chapters "Of prologues" (XVI,1), and he gives a playful rationale for their inclusion, in order that the reader may know at how many removes to take the action. I suspect it is the flirtation with frivolity in this as in the other first chapters that irritates the readers who are unaccustomed to the comic mode of presentation. But it is a feigned frivolity that causes the narrator to offer himself congratulations "for having first established these several initial chapters; most of which, like modern prologues, may as properly be prefixed to any other book in this history as to that which they introduce, or indeed to any other history as to this." For among the absurdly reasonable causes Fielding gives for the inclusion of these chapters, is the reason which in various forms and under various guises he has brought forward before: the chapters are apéritifs, "in which the critic will always be sure of meeting with something that may serve as a whetstone to his noble spirit; so that he may fall with a more hungry appetite for censure on the history itself."

To take the role of the narrator in its most obvious and explicit sense is to regard Fielding as historian. At the beginning of Book II, he goes over some ground with which readers of *Joseph Andrews* are already familiar. The chapter, "Showing what kind of a history this is; what it is like, and what it is not like," has its analogue in *Joseph Andrews.* Here, as in the earlier novel, Fielding distinguishes between the two kinds of history, the chronicle, wherein the writer "seems to think himself obliged to keep even pace with time, whose amanuensis he is"; and the history in which is disclosed "the revolutions of countries." That is, he will fix upon what is important and deal with such areas exhaustively.

> When any extraordinary scene presents itself (as we trust will often be the case), we shall spare no pains nor paper to open it at large to our reader; but if whole years should pass without producing anything worthy his notice, we shall not be afraid of a chasm in our history, but shall hasten on to matters of consequence, and leave such periods of time totally unobserved.

To apply this theory at all requires that the historian elevate himself beyond the level of time's amanuensis. He is no longer a slave but an artist. The "pure historian" has to deal with what has actually happened, but he is by this theory given leave to let his imagination play over the events of the past until he can assess and express their significance. For it was significance that the Augustans were seeking: they were concerned with the meaning of history. As Herbert Davis points out:

> Their constant preoccupation with the function of history, their study of classical and French and Italian historians, their ability to appeal to an audience who would understand their references to persons and events in classical history as parallels to guide their judgments in current political controversies—all this contributed more than is generally realized to the achievement of the great historians of the second half of the century.[5]

But Fielding, even as historian, is freer, and, while recognizing his obligation to be faithful to human nature, he makes of human probabilities a pattern of contrivance: design and distance gladden the heart.[6]

And it is as an historian that Fielding disposes of time at the beginning of the following book (III,1), the title of the prefatory chapter being, "Containing little or nothing." By the rules which he laid down at the beginning of the second book, this title is perfectly correct, and the reader has been prepared for what happens here after some preliminary fanfare: what happens is that Fielding passes over a dozen years halfway through the final sentence of the chapter and blandly asserts that he is going to "bring forth our hero, at about fourteen years of age, not questioning that many have been long impatient to be introduced to his acquaintance."

Of course, it was no new thing in the middle of the eighteenth century to write history synthetically rather than chronically. Nor was Fielding breaking new ground in fiction when he passed over large stretches of time in order to deal with his characters emphatically. Defoe, that in-

---

[5] "The Augustan Conception of History," in J. A. Mazzeo, ed., *Reason and the Imagination* (London, 1962), p. 214.

[6] In this sense also Fielding was a man of his own time, since as historian he wished to extend the boundaries of history beyond the realms to which it had been confined, the realms of politics and morals. See Professor Davis's essay, p. 229.

veterate and incorrigible journalist, was a master of emphasis—and one of the reasons for the success of the apparently artless *Moll Flanders* is just Defoe's ability to dismiss years in a sentence or two. Thus when Moll is married to her London business friend, she is perfectly secure and therefore as a fictional character uninteresting. So Defoe compresses several years into several inches, disposes—by death—of the husband, and in effect sends Moll out again to brave the world, alone. The significance, therefore, of Fielding's little essay in criticism at the beginning of Book III lies in Fielding's sophistication rather than his simplicity, and in his assumption that his audience is possessed, as he says, of "true sagacity," so that the highly civilized light of comedy shines upon the festive history of Tom Jones.

Before introducing Sophia—with, not incidentally, a flourish of high-flown language[7]—at the beginning of Book IV, Fielding writes a chapter in which the ornamental framework for her entrance is constructed with elaborate care. In the opening paragraph of this first chapter, Fielding as usual dissociates himself from the composers of "those idle romances which are filled with monsters, the productions, not of nature, but of distempered brains." He is going to be truthful, and to be truthful is, in part, to provide refreshment: "we have taken every occasion of interspersing through the whole sundry similes, descriptions, and other kind of poetical embellishments."

One way of interpreting this announcement is to suppose that Fielding is going to tell the truth and moreover make it palatable, to sweeten the moral pill. But the palatability is essential, not eccentric. The playful air is crucial melody. Here, at least, with almost rococo elegance and artificiality—rendered artificial when he compares himself as narrator to a manager of a playhouse, and even more elaborately to the maker of a pageant like the pageant of the Lord Mayor—who "contracts a good deal of that reverence which attends him through the year, by the several pageants which precede his pomp": here, at least, Fielding goes far to make the entrance of Sophia operatically and thus festively satisfying. Typically, the humblest realism is put cheek-by-jowl with the most outrageous splendor. He speaks of

> the custom of sending on a basket-woman, who is to precede the pomp at a coronation, and to strew the stage with flowers, before the great personages begin their procession. The ancients would certainly have invoked the goddess Flora for this purpose, and it would have been no difficulty

[7] Ian Watt is, it seems to me, writing autobiography rather than criticism when he says: "Sophia never wholly recovers from so artificial an introduction, or at least never wholly disengages herself from the ironical attitude which it has induced" (*The Rise of the Novel*, pp. 254f.). But it is Fielding who induces the ironical attitude, openly and deliberately, in the first chapter of the book; Sophia appears, with all the rhetorical flourishes for which Fielding has prepared us, in Chapter II.

for their priests or politicians to have persuaded the people of the real presence of the deity, though a plain mortal had personated her and performed her office. But we have no such design of imposing on our reader; and therefore those who object to the heathen theology may, if they please, change our goddess into the above-mentioned basket-woman.

As in the first chapter of Book II, Fielding in the corresponding preface to Book V insists that it is his privilege as author to make his own rules. As the head of "all prosai-comi-epic writing," he can refuse to explain why he has written prefatory essays for each of the books of *Tom Jones*. He cavils, as do practically all of his contemporaries—it was common form in the eighteenth century and has been so ever since—at the arrogance of critics, who would prescribe the rules to artists, rather than acting as clerks. And then, after this rather intimidating series of preliminaries, he disarms the reader when he says that he will "waive all the privilege above contended for, and proceed to lay before the reader the reasons which have induced us to intersperse these several digressive essays in the course of this work."

The heart of the matter is what he calls the principle of contrast, and although Fielding says that contrast "may probably have a large share in constituting in us the idea of all beauty, as well natural as artificial," it is—I think—the artificiality of the device of the opening chapters which appeals to Fielding, and no doubt to his readers. In discussing *Joseph Andrews* I have argued that Fielding's framing and reframing of even quite horrific episodes, such as that of the robbery of Joseph, has the effect of making them morally bearable, and, when seen at some distance, amusing. The same observation applies to *Tom Jones* as well, and one of the chief (though not in fact the only) framing devices is that of the preliminary chapters—as, I think, a pair of sentences here indicates Fielding himself believed. "Most artists," he says, "have this secret [the principle of contrast] in practice, though some, perhaps, have not much studied the theory. The jeweler knows that the finest brilliant requires a foil; and the painter, by the contrast of his figures, often acquires great applause." This is no doubt what Jane Austen meant when she offered some criticism of her own performance in *Pride and Prejudice*. "The work," she wrote to her sister in a celebrated letter,

> is rather too light, and bright, and sparkling; it wants shade; it wants to be stretched out here and there with a long chapter of sense, if it could be had; if not, of solemn specious nonsense, about something unconnected with the story; an essay on writing, a critique on Sir Walter Scott, or the history of Buonaparte, or anything that would form a contrast, and bring the reader with increased delight to the playfulness and epigrammatism of the general style.[8]

[8] February 4, 1813, in R. W. Chapman, ed., *Jane Austen's Letters to Her Sister Cassandra and Others* (2nd ed., London, 1952), pp. 299f.

Fielding, in fact, taught Jane Austen something about playfulness and something about how to write a novel.

Almost precisely halfway through *Tom Jones* Fielding takes the opportunity, in the preface to Book IX, to insist that he is to be taken seriously. And what is interesting about this chapter is the special sense in which Fielding is making his insistence. "Of those who lawfully may, and of those who may not, write such histories as this" contains a familiar diatribe against the mendacity of the novel and romance writers, together with a considered list of qualifications which Fielding regards as desirable for "this order of historians." Moreover, the chapter is crucially placed, for the previous book ends with the sombre and not unchallenged conclusion of the tale of the Man of the Hill; and what follows hard upon the introductory chapter is the melodrama and farce of the Battle of Upton, including its rawly comic consequences—the most outstanding of which is Mrs. Waters's successful assault, by way of mock-heroic ogling, upon Tom's all too receptive and yielding virtue. The course of the action which succeeds this introductory chapter does therefore establish the scale in which it is to be understood.

In the preface itself, Fielding sets forth three qualifications which, he says, are necessary for the kind of writing which in *Tom Jones* he has undertaken: genius, which consists of invention (and this is neither more nor less than "a quick and sagacious penetration into the true essence of all the objects of our contemplation") and judgment; second, learning—both erudition, and the sort of learning that can only be obtained by conversation; finally, a good heart. The divergence, or perhaps I should say departure, from Horace does not appear until Fielding considers this third point, for he invites us to enlarge the boundaries of our sympathy, so as to include the ridiculous, and then to put the whole chapter into a focus that will enable us to begin to enter upon an account of the action of Book IX in a spirit of rejoicing. "In reality," Fielding writes as his paraphrase of and gloss upon Horace,

> no man can paint a distress well which he doth not feel while he is painting it; nor do I doubt but that the most pathetic and affecting scenes have been writ with tears. In the same manner it is with the ridiculous. I am convinced I never make my reader laugh heartily but where I have laughed before him; unless it should happen at any time that instead of laughing with me he should be inclined to laugh at me. Perhaps this might have been the case at some passages in this chapter, from which apprehension I will here put an end to it.

The final third of *Tom Jones* is set in London, and throughout this last act of the book is the agreeable expectation, whatever apparently frightful incidents may be taking place, that a happy ending is in prospect. Appropriately, therefore, the chapter which prefaces the first book (Book

XIII) of this final section of the novel, presents Fielding in the guise of a
clown. The entire chapter, which is called "An invocation," is an apos-
trophe to a succession of authors' helps—Fame, Fortune, Genius, Humanity, Learning, and Experience—ranging in tone from Miltonic
grandeur to the prose of common day.

> Come, bright love of fame, inspire my glowing breast:
> Not thee I call, who, over swelling tides. . . .

It is almost blank verse with which Fielding begins, and he makes the
most of this elevation of tone, for his own comic purposes; after completing the invocation to Fame he turns to Fortune, "thou, much plumper
dame, whom no airy forms nor phantoms of imagination clothe; whom
the well-seasoned beef, and pudding richly stained with plums, delight."
This is the hearty Fielding, all right. But it is not all joint and York-
shire: tenderness—even tenderness—breaks in. In apostrophizing Fame,
he remembers his first wife: "Foretell me that some tender maid, whose
grandmother is yet unborn, hereafter, when, under the fictitious name
of Sophia, she reads the real worth which once existed in my Charlotte,
shall from her sympathetic breast send forth the heaving sigh." To me
this combination of heartiness and sentiment, cumbersome though it may
be here, exactly defines the moral status of *Tom Jones*: a highly organized,
tightly woven artistic recreation of the materials of "Nature"—all done
for a festive reason. To celebrate is to make life, and even death, endurable. Nor does Fielding underestimate the enormity of his undertaking,
and at the end of his individual apostrophes he makes a collective invocation, for "without all your assistance, [the task] will, I find, be too
heavy for me to support. But if you all smile on my labors I hope still to
bring them to a happy conclusion."

The preface to the eighteenth and last book of *Tom Jones,* which
Fielding calls "A farewell to the reader," casts the reader and Fielding
himself as "fellow travelers in a stagecoach": such is the comic posture
in which he would put himself and ourselves at the last. And he makes
fresh use of this well-worn comparison. He says that at the end of a journey it is "well known that all jokes and raillery are at this time laid aside;
whatever characters any of the passengers have for the jest-sake personated on the road are now thrown off, and the conversation is usually
plain and serious." This preface thus warns the reader that something
especially ludicrous or farcical or ridiculous is to follow; and in chapter
2, "Containing a very tragical incident," Partridge comes in and tells
Tom, "You have been abed with your own mother." It is the most ludicrous strand of false denouement and as such the most superb of all
demonstrations of Fielding's mastery over his novel—excepting only the
brilliance with which all the resolutions are achieved in the last book of
Fielding's masterwork: this is nothing less than a comic glory. But it is

the achiever as much as the achievement that compels our respect and admiration. As Wayne Booth puts it, in *Tom Jones* "the narrator becomes a rich and provocative chorus. It is his wisdom and learning and benevolence that permeate the world of the book, set its comic tone between the extremes of sentimental indulgence and scornful indignation, and in a sense redeem Tom's world of hypocrites and fools.⁹

⁹ *The Rhetoric of Fiction*, p. 217. [See p. 94 of this volume.]

The Plot of *Tom Jones*

by R. S. Crane

I

Of all the plots constructed by English novelists that of *Tom Jones* has probably elicited the most unqualified praise. There is "no fable whatever," according to Fielding's first biographer, that "affords, in its solution, such artful states of suspence, such beautiful turns of surprise, such unexpected incidents, and such sudden discoveries, sometimes apparently embarrassing, but always promising the catastrophe, and eventually promoting the completion of the whole." [1] Not since the days of Homer, it seemed to James Beattie, had the world seen "a more artful epick fable." "The characters and adventures are wonderfully diversified: yet the circumstances are all so natural, and rise so easily from one another, and co-operate with so much regularity in bringing on, even while they seem to retard, the catastrophe, that the curiosity of the reader . . . grows more and more impatient as the story advances, till at last it becomes downright anxiety. And when we get to the end . . . we are amazed to find, that of so many incidents there should be so few superfluous; that in such variety of fiction there should be so great probability; and that so complex a tale should be perspicuously conducted, and with perfect unity of design." [2] These are typical of the eulogies that preceded and were summed up in Coleridge's famous verdict in 1834: "What a master of composition Fielding was! Upon my word, I think the *Œdipus Tyrannus*, *The Alchemist*, and *Tom Jones*, the three most perfect plots ever planned." [3] More recent writers have tended to speak less hyperbolically and, like Scott, to insist that "even the high praise due to the construction and arrangement of the story is inferior to that claimed by

"*The Plot of* Tom Jones" *by R. S. Crane. From* The Journal of General Education, *IV (January, 1950), 112–30. Copyright © 1950 by Pennsylvania State University. Reprinted by permission of the publishers, The Pennsylvania State University Press.*

[1] Arthur Murphy (1762), quoted in Frederic T. Blanchard, *Fielding the Novelist: A Study in Historical Criticism* (New Haven, 1926), p. 161.

[2] *Dissertations Moral and Critical* (1783), quoted in Blanchard, *op. cit.*, pp. 222–23.

[3] *Ibid.*, pp. 320-21.

the truth, force, and spirit of the characters." [4] but it is hard to think of any important modern discussion of the novel that does not contain at least a few sentences on Fielding's "ever-to-be-praised skill as an architect of plot." [5]

The question I wish to raise concerns not the justice of any of these estimates but rather the nature and critical adequacy of the conception of plot in general and of the plot of *Tom Jones* in particular that under-lies most if not all of them. Now it is a striking fact that in all the more extended discussions of Fielding's masterpiece since 1749 the considera-tion of the plot has constituted merely one topic among several others, and a topic, moreover, so detached from the rest that once it is disposed of the consideration of the remaining elements of character, thought, diction, and narrative technique invariably proceeds without further reference to it. The characters are indeed agents of the story, but their values are assessed apart from this, in terms sometimes of their degrees of conformity to standards of characterization in literature generally, some-times of the conceptions of morality they embody, sometimes of their rela-tion to Fielding's experiences or prejudices, sometimes of their reflection, taken collectively, of the England of their time. The other elements are isolated similarly, both from the plot and from one another: what is found important in the thought, whether of the characters or of the nar-rator, is normally not its function as an artistic device but its doctrinal content as a sign of the "philosophy" of Fielding; the style and the ironi-cal tone of the narrative are frequently praised, but in relation solely to what they contribute to the general literary satisfaction of the reader; and, what is perhaps more significant, the wonderful comic force of the novel, which all have delighted to commend, is assumed to be independ-ent of the plot and a matter exclusively of particular incidents, of the characters of some, but not all, of the persons, and of occasional passages of burlesque or witty writing.

All this points to a strictly limited definition of plot as something that can be abstracted, for critical purposes, from the moral qualities of the characters and the operations of their thought. This something is merely the material continuity of the story considered in relation to the general pleasure we take in any fiction when our curiosity about the impending events is aroused, sustained, and then satisfied to a degree or in a manner we could not anticipate. A plot in this sense—the sense in which modern

---

[4] *Ibid.*, p. 327.

[5] The phrase is Oliver Elton's in *A Survey of English Literature, 1730–1780* (New York, 1928), I, 195. Cf. also Wilbur L. Cross, *The History of Henry Fielding* (New Haven, 1918), II, 160–61; Aurélien Digeon, *Les Romans de Fielding* (Paris, 1923), pp. 210–16; Elizabeth Jenkins, *Henry Fielding* (London, 1947), pp. 57–58; and George Sherburn, in *A Literary History of England,* ed. Albert C. Baugh (New York and London, 1948), pp. 957–58.

novelists pride themselves on having got rid of plot—can be pronounced good in terms simply of the variety of incidents it contains, the amount of suspense and surprise it evokes, and the ingenuity with which all the happenings in the beginning and middle are made to contribute to the resolution at the end. Given the definition, indeed, no other criteria are possible, and no others have been used by any of the critics of *Tom Jones* since the eighteenth century who have declared its plot to be one of the most perfect ever planned. They have uniformly judged it as interesting story merely—and this whether, as by most of the earlier writers, "the felicitous contrivance and happy extrication of the story" is taken to be the chief "beauty" of the novel or whether, as generally nowadays, preference is given to its qualities of character and thought. It is clearly of plot in no completer sense than this that Oliver Elton is thinking when he remarks that, although some "have cared little for this particular excellence, and think only of Partridge, timorous, credulous, garrulous, faithful, and an injured man; of Squire Western, and of the night at Upton, and of wit and humour everywhere," still "the common reader, for whom Fielding wrote, cares a great deal, and cares rightly, for plot; and so did Sophocles." [6]

Now it is evident that when plot is conceived thus narrowly, in abstraction from the peculiar characters and mental processes of the agents, it must necessarily have, for the critic, only a relatively external and non-functional relation to the other parts of the work. That is why, in most discussions of *Tom Jones,* the literary treatment of the plot (as distinguished from mere summary of the happenings) is restricted to the kind of enthusiastic general appreciation of which I have given some examples, supplemented by more particular remarks on various episodes, notably those of the Man of the Hill and of Mrs. Fitzpatrick, which appear to do little to advance the action. The plot, in these discussions, is simply one of many sources of interest and pleasure afforded by a novel peculiarly rich in pleasurable and interesting things, and the problem of its function with respect to the other ingredients is evaded altogether. Occasionally, it is true, the question has been faced; but even in those critics, like W. L. Cross and Oliver Elton, who have made it most explicit, the formulas suggested never give to the plot of *Tom Jones* the status of more than an external and enveloping form in relation to which the rest of the novel is content. It is not, as they see it, an end but a means, and they describe it variously, having no language but metaphor for the purpose, as a "framework" in which character (which is Fielding's "real 'bill of fare' ") is "set"; as a device, essentially "artificial," for bringing on the stage "real men and women"; as a "mere mechanism,"

6 *Op. cit.,* I, 195.

which, except now and then in the last two books, "does not obtrude," for keeping readers alert through six volumes.[7]

I do not believe, however, that it is necessary to remain content with this very limited and abstract definition of plot or with the miscellaneous and fragmentized criticism of *Tom Jones* that has always followed from it. I shall assume that any novel or drama is a composite of three elements, which unite to determine its character and effect—the things that are imitated (or "rendered") in it, the linguistic medium in which they are imitated, and the manner or technique of imitation; and I shall assume further that the things imitated necessarily involve human beings interacting with one another in ways determined by, and in turn affecting, their moral characters and their states of mind (i.e., their reasonings, emotions, and attitudes). If this is granted, we may say that the plot of any novel or drama is the particular temporal synthesis effected by the writer among the elements of action, character, and thought that constitute the matter of his invention. It is impossible, therefore, to state adequately what any plot is unless we include in our formula all three of the elements or causes of which the plot is the synthesis; and it follows also that plots may differ in structure according as one or another of the three causal ingredients is taken as the synthesizing principle. There are, thus, plots of action, plots of character, and plots of thought. In the first, the synthesizing principle is a completed change, gradual or sudden, in the fortunes of the protagonist, determined and effected by character and thought (as in *Œdipus* and James's *The Ambassadors*); in the second, the principle is a completed process of change in the moral character of the protagonist, precipitated or molded by action and made manifest both in it and in thought and feeling (as in Thackeray's *Pendennis*); in the third, the principle is a completed process of change in the thought of the protagonist and consequently in his feelings, conditioned and directed by character and action (as in Pater's *Marius the Epicurean*). All these types of construction, and not merely the first, are plots in the meaning of our definition; and it is mainly, perhaps, because most of the familiar classic plots, including that of *Tom Jones*, have been of the first kind that so many critics have tended to reduce plot to action alone.[8]

If this is granted, we may go further. For a plot, in the enlarged sense here given to the term, is not merely a particular synthesis of particular materials of character, thought, and action, but such a synthesis endowed

---

[7] Cross, *op. cit.*, II, 159–61; Elton, *op. cit.*, I, 195–96.

[8] This accounts in large part, I think, for the depreciation of "plot" in E. M. Forster's *Aspects of the Novel*, and for his notion of a rivalry between "plot" and "character," in which one or the other may "triumph."

necessarily, because it imitates in words a sequence of human activities, with a certain power to affect our opinions and emotions. We are bound, as we read or listen, to form expectations about what is coming and to feel more or less determinate desires relatively to our expectations. At the very least, if we are interested at all, we desire to know what is going to happen or how the problems faced by the characters are going to be solved. This is a necessary condition of our pleasure in all plots, and there are many good ones—in the classics of pure detective fiction, for example—the power of which depends almost exclusively on the pleasure we take in inferring progressively, from complex or ambiguous signs, the true state of affairs. For some readers and even some critics this would seem to be the chief source of delight in many plots that have obviously been constructed on more specific principles: not only *Tom Jones*, as we have seen, but *Œdipus* has been praised as a mystery story, and it is likely that much of Henry James's popularity is due to his remarkable capacity for provoking a superior kind of inferential activity. What distinguishes all the more developed forms of imaginative literature, however, is that, though they presuppose this instinctive pleasure in learning, they go beyond it and give us plots of which the effects derive in a much more immediate way from the particular ethical qualities perceptible in their agents' characters and mental activities and in the human situations in which they are engaged. When this is the case, we cannot help becoming, in a greater or less degree, emotionally involved; for some of the characters we wish good, for others ill, and, depending on our inferences as to the events, we feel hope or fear, pity or satisfaction, or some modification of these or similar emotions. The peculiar power of any plot of this kind, as it unfolds, is a result of our state of knowledge at any point in complex interaction with our desires for the characters as morally differentiated beings; and we may be said to have grasped the plot in the full artistic sense only when we have analyzed this interplay of desires and expectations sequentially in relation to the incidents by which it is produced.

It is, of course, an essential condition of such an effect that the writer should so have combined his elements of action, character, and thought as to have achieved a complete and ordered whole, with all the parts needed to carry the protagonist, by probable or necessary stages, from the beginning to the end of his change: we should not have, otherwise, any connected series of expectations wherewith to guide our desires. In itself, however, this structure is only the matter or content of the plot and not its form; the form of the plot—in the sense of that which makes its matter into a definite artistic thing—is rather its distinctive "working or power," as the form of the plot in a tragedy, for example, is the capacity of its unified sequence of actions to effect through pity and fear a catharsis of such emotions.

But if this is granted, then certain consequences follow for the criticism of dramas and novels. It is evident, in the first place, that no artistically developed plot can be called excellent merely in terms of its unity, the number and variety of its incidents, or the extent to which it produces suspense and surprise. These are but properties of its matter, and their achievement, even to a high degree, in any particular plot does not inevitably mean that the emotional effect of the whole will not still be diffused or weak. They are, therefore, only necessary and not sufficient conditions of a good plot, the positive excellence of which depends upon the capacity of its peculiar synthesis of character, action, and thought to move our feelings powerfully and pleasurably in a certain definite way.

But this capacity, which constitutes the form of the plot, is obviously, from an artistic point of view, the most important virtue any drama or novel can have; it is that, indeed, which most sharply distinguishes works of imitation from all other kinds of literary productions. It follows, consequently, that the plot, considered formally, of any artistic work is, in relation to the work as a whole, not simply a means—a "framework" or "mere mechanism"—but rather the final end which everything in the work, if that is to be felt as a whole, must be made, directly or indirectly, to serve. For the critic, therefore, the form of the plot is a first principle, which he must grasp as clearly as possible for any work he proposes to examine before he can deal adequately with the questions raised by its parts. This does not mean that we cannot derive other relevant principles of judgment from the general causes of pleasure operative in all artistic imitations, irrespective of the particular effect, serious or comic, that is aimed at in a given kind of work. The most important of these unquestionably, is the imitative principle itself, the principle that we are in general more convinced and moved when things are "rendered" for us through probable signs than when they are given merely in "statement," without illusion, after the fashion of a scenario.[9] Critical judgments, valid enough if they are not taken absolutely, may also be drawn from considerations of the general possibilities of language as a literary medium, of the known potentialities of a given manner of representation (e.g., dramatic or narrative), and of the various conditions of suspense and surprise. We are not likely to feel keenly the emotional effect of a work in which the worse rather than the better alternatives among these different expedients are consistently chosen or chosen in crucial scenes. And the same thing can be said of works in which the thought, however

---

[9] The meaning and force of this will be clear to anyone who has compared in detail the text of *The Ambassadors* with James's preliminary synopsis of the novel (*The Notebooks of Henry James* [New York, 1947], pp. 372–415) . See also the excellent remarks of Allen Tate, apropos of *Madame Bovary*, in his "Techniques of Fiction" (*Forms of Modern Fiction*, ed. William Van O'Connor [Minneapolis, 1948], esp. pp. 37–45).

clearly serving an artistic use, is generally uninteresting or stale, or in which the characters of the agents, though right enough in conception for the intended effect, are less than adequately "done," or in which we perceive that the most has not been made of the possibilities implicit in the incidents. Such criticism of parts in terms of general principles is indispensable, but it is no substitute for—and its conclusions, affirmative as well as negative, have constantly to be checked by—the more specific kind of criticism of a work that takes the form of the plot as its starting point and then inquires how far and in what ways its peculiar power is maximized by the writer's invention and development of particular episodes, his step-by-step rendering of the characters of his people, his use and elaboration of thought, his handling of diction and imagery, and his decisions as to the order, method, scale, and point of view of his representation.

All this is implied, I think, in the general hypothesis about plot which I have been outlining here and which I now propose to illustrate further in a re-examination of the "ever-to-be-praised" plot of *Tom Jones.*

II

It is necessary to look first at its matter and to begin by asking what is the unifying idea by which this is held together. Elementary as the question is, I have not read any answers to it that do not, in one way or another, mistake one of the parts of Fielding's novel for the whole. Doubtless the most common formula is that which locates the essence of the story in the sustained concealment and final disclosure of Tom's parentage. "It is pleasant," writes Oliver Elton, "to consider *Tom Jones* as a puzzle and to see how well the plan works out." For others the most important unifying factor is the love affair of Tom and Sophia; for still others, the conflict between Tom and Blifil; for others again, the quasi-picaresque sequence of Tom's adventures with women and on the road. The novel, it is true, would be quite different in its total effect if any of these four lines of action had been left out, but it is obvious that no one of them so subsumes all the others as to justify us in considering it, even on the level of material action, as the principle of the whole. A distinctive whole there is, however, and I venture to say that it consists, not in any mere combination of these parts, but rather in the dynamic system of actions, extending throughout the novel, by which the divergent intentions and beliefs of a large number of persons of different characters and states of knowledge belonging to or somehow related to the neighboring families of the Allworthys and the Westerns are made to co-operate, with the assistance of Fortune, first to bring Tom into an incomplete and precarious union, founded on an affinity of nature in

spite of a disparity of status, with Allworthy and Sophia; then to separate
him as completely as possible from them through actions that impel
both of them, one after the other, to reverse their opinions of his character; and then, just as he seems about to fulfill the old prophecy that "he
was certainly born to be hanged," to restore them unexpectedly to him
in a more entire and stable union of both affection and fortune than he
has known before.

The unity of *Tom Jones* is contained in this formula, but only potentially; and before we can properly discuss the plot as an artistic principle
we must examine, in some detail, the intricate scheme of probabilities,
involving moral choices, mistaken judgments, and accidents of Fortune,
which bind its many parts together from the time we first see Tom in
Allworthy's bed until we leave him, calmly enjoying his double good
luck, at the end of Book XVIII.

There are three major stages in the action, the first of which, constituting in relation to the other two stages a "beginning," is complete by
chapter vii of Book V. The starting point of everything is Bridget's
scheme to provide security for both herself and her illegitimate son by
palming off Tom on Allworthy as a foundling, with the intention, however, of ultimately informing her brother of the truth. The first part of
the plan works beautifully: the affection which "the good man" at once
conceives for the child assures Tom of a proper home and upbringing,
and suspicion is diverted from his mother by Allworthy's discovery of
parents for him, first in Jenny Jones (who, as Bridget's agent, is in the
secret) and then in Partridge (who is not), and by the consequent departure of both of these from the neighborhood. In the end, too, Bridget's
second purpose is fulfilled; but meanwhile she has put both parts of her
scheme for Tom in jeopardy by her marriage (facilitated, again, by Allworthy's "penetration") with Captain Blifil. As a result, no early disclosure of Tom's true parentage is possible, and in addition the boy
acquires a potential rival, in the younger Blifil, for both the affection
and the fortune of Allworthy. On the other hand, although the intrigue
against him begins immediately after the marriage, its only result at this
stage, thanks to the goodness of Allworthy and the obvious innocence
of Tom, is to make him thought of henceforth as the son of Partridge.
This damages him in the eyes of the "world," but his status as a protégé
and heir, along with young Blifil, of the benevolent Allworthy is still
secure and will remain secure so long as his protector has no reason to
think him unworthy of his favor.

A second phase of the "beginning" opens in Book III, with the emergence of moral character in the two half-brothers. There are now, so far
as Tom is concerned, two main problems. The first has to do with his
relation to Allworthy, for whom by this time he has come to feel as
strong an affection as Allworthy has felt, and continues to feel, for him.

There can be no change on his part no matter what Allworthy does, since his feelings are based not on any opinion of interest but on the instinctive love of one good nature for another; and there can equally be no change on Allworthy's part that will lead to a separation between them unless something happens to convince him that Tom's nature is after all bad. That under certain circumstances Allworthy should be capable of such a verdict on Tom is made probable, generally, by the excessive confidence in his ability to judge of character which has led him long before to condemn Partridge, and, particularly, by his implicit and, in the face of Bridget's favoritism for Tom, even aggressive belief in the good intentions of young Blifil, as well as in the integrity of the learned men he has chosen, in his wisdom, as tutors for the two boys.

Occasions for passing judgment on Tom present themselves increasingly from his fourteenth year; and Blifil, seconded by Thwackum and Square, misses no chance of using them to blacken his character in his guardian's eyes. The occasions are given by Tom's well-intentioned but quixotic and imprudently managed actions toward Black George and his family, before and after his seduction by Molly. In the first series of these, no harm, in spite of Blifil, is done; on the contrary,. as we are told, Tom by his generosity has "rather improved than injured the affection which Mr. Allworthy was inclined to entertain for him." And it is the same at first with the actions that culminate in Tom's mistaken confession that he is the father of Molly's child; angry as Allworthy is at Tom's incontinence, he is "no less pleased with the honour and honesty of his self-accusation" and he begins "to form in his mind the same opinion of this young fellow, which, we hope, our reader may have conceived"; it is only later, after having pardoned him, that he is induced by the sophistry of Square to entertain his "first bad impression concerning Jones." But even this is not fatal to Tom: he is assured again after his injury, though with a warning for the future, that what has happened is "all forgiven and forgotten"; he remains a beneficiary, in proportion to his supposed status, in Allworthy's will; and he is thought of by Allworthy, as we learn from the latter's speech in Book V, chapter vii, as one who has "much goodness, generosity, and honour" in his temper and needs only "prudence and religion" to make him actually happy. Fortune, it is clear, is still, however hesitatingly, on the side of Tom.

The other problem concerns the attachment that has been developing meanwhile between Tom and Sophia. The basis of the attachment is again one of likeness of nature, and the function of the incidents in Books IV and V in which the two are thrown together (Tom's intervention on behalf of Black George, his rescue of Sophia and his convalescence at her house, the affair of the muff, etc.) is simply to make credible its rapid progress, in spite of Tom's initial indifference and his entanglement with Molly, to the stage of mutual recognition reached in Book V, chapter vi. From this point on, we need not expect any change in Tom's feelings toward Sophia, no matter what he may do in his character as gallant; and there is an equally strong probability, in terms of her character, that Sophia will never cease to love Tom. She is, for one thing, a better judge of persons than Allworthy and is in no danger of being deceived, as he is, by the formal appearances of virtue in Blifil and of vice in Tom. "To say the truth, Sophia, when very young, discerned that Tom, though an idle, thoughtless, rattling rascal, was nobody's enemy but his own; and that Master Blifil, though a prudent, discreet, sober young gentleman, was at the same time strongly attached to the interest only of one single person . . ." (IV,v). She has, more-over, been even more completely aware than Allworthy of Tom's affair with Molly, and yet, for all her hurt pride, she has not altered her opinion of his worth; Tom, it is evident, will have to behave, or appear to behave, much worse than this before she will decide to cast him off. In the meantime, however, their union is apparently condemned by circumstances to be one of affection only. Her father, though very fond of Tom, will not approve a marriage which offers, because of Tom's low status, so little prospect of fortune for his beloved daughter; she will not act counter to her father's wishes, even though she will not agree to marry against her own feelings; and as for Tom, though his life is now "a constant struggle between honour and inclination," he can do nothing that will injure Sophia, show ingratitude to Western, or violate his more than filial piety toward Allworthy. The only possible resolu-tion of their problem, it is plain, must be some event that will alter fundamentally Tom's position as a foundling.

Such an event is indeed impending at precisely this point in the action. For Bridget, dying, has just confided her secret to her attorney Dowling and has commanded him to carry the all-important message to Allworthy in fulfilment of the second part of her original design.

Blifil, however, aided by Fortune (which now turns temporarily against Tom), here intervenes, with two important results: immediately, that a chain of happenings is set in motion, constituting the "middle" of the plot, which leads to the complete separation of Tom from both Allworthy and Sophia; and remotely, that, when Bridget's message is at last delivered in Book XVIII, the position to which Tom is then restored is made, by reason of the delay, one of even greater security and happi-ness than would have been possible had his relationship to Allworthy become known at the time Bridget intended to reveal it.

The action from the moment when Bridget gives Dowling her message to the moment, many weeks later, when Allworthy receives it falls into three main parts. The first part begins with Allworthy's illness and ends with Tom's expulsion and Sophia's flight. The events in this stage form a single complex sequence, in which Fortune conspires with the malice and ambition of Blifil, the pride and family tyranny of the Westerns, and the easily imposed-on sense of justice of Allworthy, first to thwart the purpose of Bridget and then to turn the indiscreet manifestations of Tom's love for Allworthy and joy at his recovery and of Sophia's love for Tom into occasions for the condemnation and banishment of Tom as "an abandoned reprobate" and for the persecution of Sophia as a recalcitrant daughter. The separating action of the novel thus comes to its first major climax, with Tom now resolved, for the sake of Sophia, to renounce her and leave the country, and with Sophia, unable to endure the prospect of a marriage with Blifil, determined to seek refuge in London with her cousin Lady Bellaston, not without hopes of again seeing Tom. Blifil, now dearer than ever to Allworthy because of Tom's "ill-treatment of that good young man," has apparently triumphed, though not completely, since Sophia is still out of his grasp. In reality, he has already made his fatal mistake, the mistake that will inevitably ruin him and restore Tom if and when Allworthy discovers it; and in addition, by driving Tom out, he has made it more rather than less probable that the truth he has concealed will eventually come to light, since, besides himself, it is also known, in part or in whole, to three other persons—Partridge, Jenny Jones, and Dowling—any or all of whom it is more likely now than before that Tom will meet.

This is, in fact, what happens during the next stage of the action, all the incidents of which converge on bringing Tom into contact, first with Partridge, then with Dowling, and finally with Jenny (now Mrs. Waters). The first meeting leads to a kind of negative resolution: Tom now knows that he is not Partridge's son. From the meetings with the others, who alone, save Blifil, know the whole truth, no resolution immediately follows, being prevented in both cases by the same causes that have determined Tom's fate hitherto: in the case of Jenny by Fortune, which sees to it that there is no encounter between her and Partridge at Upton; in the case of Dowling, who is ready to sell his knowledge for a price, by Tom's quixotic disinterestedness. The crucial discovery in thus postponed, but when we consider that Tom is now known to Dowling and to Jenny (though to the latter not as Bridget's son) and that both of these now become attached to persons in the Allworthy-Western circle—Jenny to Sophia's cousin-in-law Fitzpatrick and Dowling to Blifil—it is clear that the probability of its eventually taking place, and possibly in more auspicious circumstances, is increased rather than diminished by what has occurred.

In the meantime, with the happenings at Upton, the complication has entered its last and longest and, for Tom, most distressing phase, the climax of which, at the end of Book XVI, is his receipt in prison of Sophia's letter of condemnation and dismissal. The principal villain is again Fortune, which as we have been told (V,x), "seldom doth things by halves," and which, having already robbed Tom of the good will of Allworthy, now seems bent on completing his unhappiness by using his too complaisant good nature and his capacity for indiscretion to deprive him of Sophia and perhaps even of his life. It all begins with the chapter of accidents at the inn, where, because of his gallantry to Jenny, Tom first has an angry encounter with Fitzpatrick (who is seeking his runaway wife) and then misses Sophia, who departs at once on learning of his infidelity and makes her way, in the company of Mrs. Fitzpatrick, to London and Lady Bellaston. Some harm has now been done, but not much, as Tom learns when, having pursued her to London, he finally meets her again at Lady Bellaston's and is told, in a tender scene, that what has really disturbed her has not been so much his misconduct with Jenny, which she can forgive, as Partridge's free use of her name in public.

This happy resolution, however, comes too late; for already, although with the best intentions—namely, of finding his way to Sophia—Tom has been seduced into the affair with Lady Bellaston which is his closest approach, in the novel, to a base act. The affair does indeed lead him to Sophia, but only by chance, and then under circumstances which, while they do not betray him to Sophia, turn the wrath of his new mistress against her and lead to a fresh series of efforts to separate her from Tom. The first of these, the attempted rape by Lord Fellamar, is thwarted when Western, having learned of his daughter's whereabouts, rescues her in the nick of time and carries her away to his lodgings to face another course of family persecution and threats of imminent marriage to Blifil. It is on hearing of this that Tom, his thoughts now centered wholly on Sophia in spite of his despair of ever winning her, decides to break with Lady Bellaston, and adopts the expedient for doing so without dishonor which nearly leads to his ruin. For the effect of his proposal of marriage is to draw the Lady's vengeful feelings upon himself and Sophia at once, with the result that she arranges for his kidnapping by a press gang at the same time that she makes sure that Sophia will never marry him by sending her the letter of proposal as proof of his villainy. With Sophia her scheme succeeds, so incapable of any other interpretation does the evidence seem. She is foiled, however, in her design against Tom, and once more by a delayed effect of the events at Upton. But the meeting which Fortune brings about with the still angry Fitzpatrick, though it saves Tom from being pressed into the navy, spares him only for what promises to be a worse fate.

The separating action has now come to its second major climax— much the more serious of the two for Tom, since he has not only lost Sophia as well as Allworthy but lost her, he thinks, as a direct result of his own vice and folly. He can still, if Fitzpatrick dies, be separated from

his life, but otherwise all the possibilities of harm to him contained in
his original situation have been exhausted. Not, however, all the possibilities of good; for the very same incidents proceeding from the affair at
Upton which have so far been turned by Fortune against Tom have
also had consequences which Fortune, bent upon doing nothing by
halves, may yet exploit in his favor.

The most important of these in the long run is the moral change that
has been produced by his recent experiences in Tom himself, as manifested by his break with Lady Bellaston and by his rejection of the honorable advances of Mrs. Hunt and the dishonorable advances of Mrs.
Fitzpatrick. It is not so much what he is, however, as what he is thought
to be by Allworthy and Sophia that immediately counts; and he has
had the good luck, by virtue of coming to London, of acquiring in Mrs.
Miller a character witness who knows the best as well as the worst of him
and who will at least be listened to by her old friend and benefactor Allworthy and perhaps by Sophia. There is, moreover, as a result of what has
happened, rather less danger than before that Sophia, who, in spite of her
reason, still loves Tom, will be forced to marry Blifil; for, though she is
again in the power of her family, the machinations of Lady Bellaston
have led to a conflict between the two Westerns over the rival merits of
Blifil and Lord Fellamar. Time has thus been gained for Tom; and meanwhile Allworthy and Blifil have come up to town in response to Western's
summons and have taken lodgings with Mrs. Miller. Dowling has come
too, and so also has Jenny, now living with Fitzpatrick in lieu of the wife
he has been seeking since Upton and whose whereabouts he has just
learned. All those, in short, who know Bridget's secret—and Blifil's
villainy in suppressing it at the time of her death—are now assembled,
for the first time, in close proximity to Allworthy. And then Blifil, made
overconfident by his success and believing Fitzpatrick about to die of his
wound, decides to use the opportunity afforded by the presence of Lord
Fellamar's press gang at the duel to strike one last blow at Tom.

But this time all the acts of Fortune work to the advantage of our
hero, and the resolution moves rapidly to its end, first by the reunion of
Tom with Allworthy and then by his reunion with Sophia. The first
requires a reversal of Allworthy's judgment of Tom's character and
actions at the time of his banishment. This is prepared by Mrs. Miller's
insistence upon his present goodness and the services he has rendered
her family, but the decisive event is the letter from the dying and repentant Square, which sets in a new light Tom's acts during Allworthy's
illness, although without clearly implicating Blifil. The result is to restore Tom to his foster-father's affections more or less on the footing
which he had at the beginning of Book V, but with the added circumstance that he has since suffered unjust persecution. The new Tom is
not yet fully known, or the entire extent and cause of the injuries that

have been done to him. Mrs. Miller indeed suspects, but the blindness of Allworthy prevents a discovery; and it requires a second intervention of Fortune, aided by the rashness of Blifil, to bring the revelation about. For not only does Blifil think Fitzpatrick's wound more serious that it is, but in his zeal to gather all possible evidence damaging to Tom he has made it inevitable that Jenny will come to know who Tom is, that she will at once go to Allworthy with her story, that Dowling will then be questioned, and that he, seeing where his profit now lies, will tell the whole truth about the suppression of Bridget's dying message. Thus here again Fortune has done nothing by halves, with the result that the exclusive place which Blifil has all along sought for himself in Allworthy's fortune and favor is now, with his unmasking and subsequent banishment, properly accorded to Tom. In relation to the original conditions of the action, moreover, the reversal is equally complete: Bridget's intended disclosure of her secret has at last been made, and with it both of her mistakes—of concealing Tom's parentage and then of marrying the elder Blifil—are finally canceled out.

The reunion with Sophia is likewise prepared by Mrs. Miller, who is able to convince her that Tom's letter proposing marriage to Lady Bellaston was at worst an indiscretion. But though Allworthy also intervenes on his nephew's behalf and though Western is now as violent an advocate for Tom as he has earlier been for Blifil, the resolution comes only when Sophia, faced with the repentant young man, finds once more (as after his previous affairs with Molly and Jenny) that her love for him is stronger than her injured pride and that it is now a pleasure to be able to obey her father's commands.

It is in nothing short of this total system of actions, moving by probable or necessary connections from beginning, through middle, to end, that the unity of the plot of *Tom Jones* is to be found. It is the unity, clearly, of a complex plot, built on two continuous but contrary lines of probability, both stemming from the double scheme of Bridget respecting Tom and from her marriage with Captain Blifil, and both reinforced, from Book III onward, by the combination in Tom's character of goodness and indiscretion: the one producing immediately, throughout the complication, ever more bad fortune and distress for Tom, the other at the same time preparing for him the good luck he finally comes to enjoy after the discovery and reversal in Book XVIII. It is no wonder that this "plot," in which so many incidents, involving so many surprising turns, are all subsumed so brilliantly under one principle of action, should have been praised by all those critics from the eighteenth century to the present who have had a taste for intricate and ingenious constructions of this kind.

If the plot of *Tom Jones* is still to be praised, however, it ought to be for reasons more relevant than these to the special artistic quality of the novel we continue to read. For what we have discussed so far as the "plot" is merely the abstract action of the novel as unified and made probable by its basic elements of character and thought. It is not the plot proper but only its necessary substrate, and if we are to say what the plot proper is and be able to use our account for critical purposes, we must go beyond the material system of actions—which Fielding might have had fully developed in his mind before writing a word of *Tom Jones*—and look for the formal principle which, in the novel as finally composed for readers in an ordered arrangement of paragraphs, chapters, and books, actually operates to determine our emotionalized expectations for Tom and our subsequent reactions when the hoped-for or feared events occur.

III

In stating this principle for any plot, we must consider three things: (1) the general estimate we are induced to form, by signs in the work, of the moral character and deserts of the hero, as a result of which we tend, more or less ardently, to wish for him either good or bad fortune in the end; (2) the judgments we are led similarly to make about the nature of the events that actually befall the hero or seem likely to befall him, as having either painful or pleasurable consequences for him, and this in greater or less degree and permanently or temporarily; and (3) the opinions we are made to entertain concerning the degree and kind of his responsibility for what happens to him, as being either little or great and, if the latter, the result either of his acting in full knowledge of what he is doing or of some sort of mistake. The form of a given plot is a function of the particular correlation among these three variables which the completed work is calculated to establish, consistently and progressively, in our minds; and in these terms we may say that the plot of *Tom Jones* has a pervasively comic form. The precise sense, however, in which its form is comic is a rather special one, which needs to be carefully defined.

To begin with, it is obviously a plot in which the complication generates much pain and inner suffering for the hero, as a result of misfortunes which would seem genuinely serious to any good person. He is schemed against by a villain who will not stop even at judicial murder to secure his ends, and, what is worse in his eyes, he loses the good will of the two people whom he most loves, and loses it as a consequence not simply of the machinations of his enemies but of his own mistaken acts. From near the beginning until close to the end, moreover, he is made to undergo an almost continuous series of distressing indignities: to be insulted on the score of his birth, to be forbidden the sight of

Sophia, to see her being pushed into a hated marriage with Blifil and persecuted when she refuses, to be banished abruptly from home, to be reduced to poverty and forced to take money from Lady Bellaston, to be laid in wait for by a press gang, to be compelled to run a man through in self-defense, and finally, in prison, to be faced with the prospect of a disgraceful death.

The hero, furthermore, to whom all this happens is a naturally good man—not notably virtuous, but, for all his faults, at least the equal of ourselves and of any other character in the novel in disinterestedness, generosity, and tender benevolent feeling. These traits are impressed upon us in the third book and are never obscured even in the worst of Tom's troubles in London; they are, in fact, revivified for us, just at the point when we might be most tempted to forget them, by the episodes of Anderson and of Mrs. Miller's daughter. We like Tom, therefore, even if we do not admire him, and we wish for him the good fortune with Allworthy and Sophia which he properly wishes for himself and which, in terms of his basic moral character, he deserves to get. We follow him through his troubles and distresses, consequently, with a desire that he will eventually be delivered from them and reunited to his friend and mistress, and this all the more when, at the climax of his diffi-culties, we see him acting, for the first time, in a way we can entirely approve; in the end, when our wishes for him are unexpectedly realized, and to a fuller degree than we had anticipated, we feel some of the joy which Fielding says (XVIII, xiii) was then felt by the principal charac-ters themselves. "All were happy, but those the most who had been most unhappy before. Their former sufferings and fears gave such a relish to their felicity as even love and fortune, in their fullest flow, could not have given without the advantage of such a comparison."

Having conceived a plot in which so sympathetic a character is sub-jected in the complication to experiences so painful, it would have been relatively easy for Fielding to write a novel similar in form to his *Amelia,* that is to say, a tragi-comedy of common life designed to arouse and then to dissipate, by a sudden happy resolution, emotions of fear and pity for his hero and of indignation toward his enemies. There is, in-deed, an even greater material basis for such an effect in *Tom Jones* than in the later novel: the evils that threaten Tom and the indignities he undergoes are, in the abstract, more serious than anything Booth has to fear, and the same thing is true of the persecutions endured by Sophia as compared with those which Amelia is made to suffer. And yet nothing is more evident than that, whereas the emotions awakened in us by the distresses of Booth and Amelia are the graver emotions of anxiety and compassion that yield what Fielding calls "the pleasure of tenderness," [10]

[10] *Amelia,* III, i.

our feelings for Tom and Sophia, as we anticipate or view in actuality the greater evils that befall them prior to the final discovery, partake only in the mildest degree of this painful quality. We do not actively fear for or pity either of them, and our indignation at the actions of their enemies—even the actions of Blifil—never develops into a sustained punitive response.

Nor is the reason for this hard to find. It is generally the case that whatever tends to minimize our fear in a plot that involves threats of undeserved misfortune for the sympathetic characters tends also to minimize our pity when the misfortune occurs and likewise our indignation against the doers of the evil; and fear for Tom and Sophia as they move toward the successive climaxes of their troubles is prevented from becoming a predominant emotion in the complication of *Tom Jones* chiefly by two things.

The first is our perception, which in each case grows stronger as the novel proceeds, that the persons whose actions threaten serious consequences for the hero and heroine are all persons for whom, though in varying degrees, we are bound to feel a certain contempt. The most formidable of them all is of course Blifil. As a villain, however, he is no Iago but merely a clever opportunist who is likely to overreach himself (as the failure of his first schemes shows) and whose power of harm depends entirely on the blindness of Allworthy; he deceives Tom only temporarily and Sophia and Mrs. Miller not at all; and after we have seen the display of his personal ineptitude in the proposal scene with Sophia, we are prepared to wait, without too much active suspense, for his final showing-up. Blifil is too coldly selfish, perhaps, to strike us as positively ridiculous, but in the characters of the other agents of misfortune the comic strain is clear. It is most obvious, needless to say, in Squire Western and his sister: who can really fear that the persecutions directed against the determined and resourceful Sophia by such a blundering pair of tyrants can ever issue in serious harm? For Allworthy, too, in spite of his excellent principles, it is hard for us to maintain entire respect; we should certainly take more seriously his condemnation of Tom in Book VI had we not become accustomed, as a result of earlier incidents in the novel, to smile at a man who could believe in the goodness of the two Blifils and whose pride in his own judgment could make him dispose so precipitously of Jenny and Partridge. There are evident comic traits also in all the persons who cause trouble for Tom and Sophia in the later part of the action: in Dowling, the man always in a hurry; in Lady Bellaston, the great dame who pursues a plebeian with frenzied letters and nocturnal visits to his lodgings; in Lord Fellamar, the half-hearted rake; in Fitzpatrick, the unfaithful but jealous husband who will not believe the evidence of his own eyes. In respect of her relations with Tom, though not otherwise, Sophia, too, must be added to the list, as a virtuous girl with a proper amount of spirit (not to say vanity) whose good resolutions against Tom never survive for long in the presence of her lover. These are all manifestations of the ineffectual or ridiculous in a plot in which the impending events are materially painful, and they contribute, on the principle that we fear less or not at all when the agents of harm to a hero are more or less laughable persons, to induce in us a general feeling of confidence that matters are not really as serious as they appear.

A second ground of security lies in the nature of the probabilities for future action that are made evident progressively as the novel unfolds. From the beginning until the final capitulation of Sophia, the successive incidents constantly bring forth new and unexpected complications, each seemingly fraught with more suffering for Tom than the last; but as we read we instinctively infer from past occurrences to what will probably happen next or in the end, and what steadily cumulates in this way, in spite of the gradual worsening of Tom's situation, is an opinion that, since nothing irreparable has so far happened to him, nothing ever will. In one sense—that which relates to its material events—the action becomes more and more serious as it moves to its climax, in another sense—that which relates to our expectations—less and less serious; and I think that any close reader who keeps in mind the earlier parts of the novel as he attends to the later is inevitably made aware of this, with the result that, though his interest mounts, his fear increasingly declines. We come thus to the first climax in Book VI recalling such things as Jenny's assurance to Allworthy that she will someday make known the whole truth, the sudden reversal of the elder Blifil's sinister plans, the collapse, after initial success, of young Blifil's first schemes against Tom, and Tom's return to favor with Allworthy after the incident of Molly's arrest; and all these memories inevitably operate to check the rise of any long-range apprehensions. And it is the same, too, with the second and apparently much more serious climax at the end of Book XVI, when Tom, dismissed by Sophia, lies in prison awaiting the death of Fitzpatrick, who has been given up by his surgeon: we cannot but remember how, in the affairs of Molly and then of Mrs. Waters, Sophia has more than once demonstrated her inability to inflict any great or prolonged punishment on Tom for his sins with other women and how, on the occasion of Allworthy's illness in Book V, the outcome had completely disappointed the gloomy predictions of the doctor.

The attenuation, in these ways, of fear, pity, and indignation is a necessary condition of the peculiar comic pleasure which is the form of the plot in *Tom Jones,* but it is only a negative and hence not a sufficient condition. A comic effect of any kind would be impossible if we took Tom's increasingly bad prospects with the same seriousness as he himself takes them, but what in a positive sense makes Fielding's plot comic is the combination of this feeling of security with our perception of the decisive role which Tom's own blunders are made to play, consistently, in the genesis of all the major difficulties into which he is successively brought—always, of course, with the eager assistance of Fortune and of the malice or misunderstanding of others. The importance of this becomes clear at once when we consider how much trouble he would have spared himself had he not mistaken his seduction by Molly for a seduction of her by him; had he not got drunk when he learned of Allworthy's recovery or fought with Blifil and Thwackum; had he not suggested to Western that he be allowed to plead Blifil's case with Sophia; had he not allowed himself to be seduced by Jenny at Upton; had he not thought that his very love for Sophia, to say nothing of his gallantry, required him "to keep well" with the lady at the masquerade; and, lastly, had he not accepted so uncritically Nightingale's scheme for compelling her to break off the affair.

The truth is that each successive stage of the plot up to the beginning of the denouement in Book XVII is precipitated by a fresh act of imprudence or indiscretion on the part of Tom, for which he is sooner or later made to suffer not only in his fortune but his feelings, until, in the resolution of each sequence, he discovers that the consequences of his folly are after all not so serious as he has feared. This characteristic pattern emerges, even before the start of the complication proper, in the episode of Tom's relations with Molly and Sophia in Book IV and the first part of Book V; it dominates the prolonged suspense of his relations with Allworthy from the time of the latter's illness to the final discovery; and it determines the course of his troubles with Sophia from Upton to the meeting in London and from the ill-conceived proposal scheme to her sudden surrender at the end.

The comic pleasure all this gives us is certainly not of the same kind as that produced by such classic comic plots as (say) Ben Jonson's *The Silent Woman* or, to take a more extreme instance of the type, his *Volpone,* in which a morally despicable person is made, by reason of his own folly or lapse from cleverness, to suffer a humiliating and, to him, though not to others, painful reversal of fortune. The comedy of Blifil is indeed of this simple punitive kind,[11] but our suspense concerning Blifil is only in a secondary way determinative of the effect of Fielding's novel, and the comedy of Tom and hence of the plot as a whole is of a different sort. It is not simple comedy but mixed, the peculiar power of which depends upon the fact that the mistaken acts of the hero which principally excite our amusement are the acts of a man for whom throughout the plot we entertain sympathetic feelings

---

[11] I borrow this term from Elder Olson's "An Outline of Poetic Theory," in *Critiques and Essays in Criticism, 1920–1948,* ed. Robert W. Stallman (New York, 1949), p. 273.

because of the general goodness of his character: we do not want, therefore, to see him suffer any permanent indignity or humiliation, and
we never cease to wish good fortune for him in the end. This favorable
attitude, moreover, is not contradicted by anything in the acts themselves from which his troubles spring. We perceive that in successive
situations involving threats to his fortune or peace of mind, he invariably does some imprudent or foolish thing, which cannot fail, the circumstances being what, in our superior knowledge, we see them to be,
to result for him in painful embarrassment and regret; but we realize
that his blunders arise from no permanent weakness of character but
are merely the natural errors of judgment, easily corrigible in the future,
of an inexperienced and too impulsively generous and gallant young
man. We look forward to the probable consequences of his indiscretions, therefore, with a certain anticipatory reluctance and apprehension
—a kind of faint alarm which is the comic analogue of fear; it is some
such feeling, I think, that we experience, if only momentarily, when
Tom gets drunk and goes into the wood with Molly and when, much
later, he sends his proposal letter to Lady Bellaston. We know that
trouble, more trouble than the young man either foresees or deserves,
is in store for him as a result of what he has done, and since, foolish
as he is, we favor him against his enemies, the expectation of his inevitable suffering cannot be purely and simply pleasant.

And yet the expectation is never really painful in any positive degree,
and it is kept from becoming so by our counter-expectation, established
by the devices I have mentioned, that, however acute may be Tom's
consequent sufferings, his mistakes will not issue in any permanent
frustration of our wishes for his good. In this security that no genuine
harm has been done, we can view his present distresses—as when he
anguishes over the wrong he thinks he has done to Molly, or finds Sophia's muff in his bed at Upton or receives her letter—as the deserved
consequences of erroneous actions for which any good man would
naturally feel embarrassment or shame. We do not therefore pity him in
these moments, for all his self-accusations and cries of despair, but rather,
in a quiet way, laugh at him as a man who has behaved ridiculously or
beneath himself and is now being properly punished. And our comic
pleasure continues into the subsequent resolving scenes—the discovery
of Molly in bed with Square, the meeting with Sophia in London, and
the final anticlimax of her agreement to marry him the next morning—
when it appears that Tom has after all worried himself overmuch; for
we now see that he has been doubly ridiculous, at first in not taking his
situation seriously enough and then in taking it more seriously than he
should. But Tom is a good man, and we expect him to get better, and
so our amused reaction to his sufferings lacks entirely the punitive quality that characterizes comedy of the Jonsonian type. If the anticipatory

emotion is a mild shudder of apprehension, the climactic emotion—the comic analogue of pity—is a kind of friendly mirth at his expense ("poor Tom," we say to ourselves), which easily modulates, in the happy denouement, into unsentimental rejoicing at his not entirely deserved good fortune.

This, however, is not quite all; for not only does Tom's final good fortune seem to us at least partly undeserved in terms of his own behavior, but we realize, when we look back from the end upon the long course of the action, that he has, in truth, needed all the luck that has been his. Again and again he has been on the verge of genuinely serious disaster; and, though we expect him to survive and hence do not fear for him in prospect, we perceive, at the resolution of each of his major predicaments, that there has been something of a hairbreadth quality in his escape. The cards have indeed been stacked against him; from the beginning to the ultimate discovery, he has been a young man whose lack of security and imprudence more than offset his natural goodness, living in a world in which the majority of people are ill-natured and selfish, and some of them actively malicious, and in which the few good persons are easily imposed upon by appearances. It is against this background of the potentially serious—more than ever prominent in the London scenes—that the story of Tom's repeated indiscretions is made to unfold, with the result that though, as I have argued, the pleasure remains consistently comic, its quality is never quite that of the merely amiable comedy, based likewise upon the blunders of sympathetic protagonists, of such works as *She Stoops To Conquer* or *The Rivals*. We are not disposed to feel, when we are done laughing at Tom, that all is right with the world or that we can count on Fortune always intervening, in the same gratifying way, on behalf of the good.

IV

This or something very close to this, I think, is the intended "working or power" of *Tom Jones,* and the primary question for the critic concerns the extent to which Fielding's handling of the constituent parts of the novel is calculated to sustain and maximize this special pleasure which is its form.

It must be said that he sometimes fails. There are no perfect works of art, and, though many of the faults that have been found in *Tom Jones* are faults only on the supposition that it should have been another kind of novel, still enough real shortcomings remain to keep one's enthusiasm for Fielding's achievement within reasonable bounds. There are not infrequent *longueurs,* notably in the Man of the Hill's story (whatever positive values this may have), in Mrs. Fitzpatrick's narrative to Sophia (useful as this is in itself), in the episode of Tom's encounter with the gypsies, and in the final complications of the Nightingale affair. With the best will in the world, too, it is impossible not to be shocked by Tom's acceptance of fifty pounds from Lady Bellaston on the night of his first meeting with her at the masquerade and his subsequent emergence as "one of the best-dressed men about town"; it is necessary, no doubt, that he should now fall lower than ever before, but surely not so low as to make it hard for us to infer his act from our previous knowledge of his character and of the rather modest limits hitherto of his financial need; for the moment at least, a different Tom is before our eyes. And there are also more general faults. The narrator, for one thing, though it is well that he should intrude, perhaps intrudes too much in a purely ornamental way; the introductory essays, thus, while we should not like to lose them from the canon of Fielding's writings, serve only occasionally the function of chorus, and the returns from them, even as embellishment, begin to diminish before the end. What chiefly strikes the modern reader, however, is the extent of Fielding's reliance, in the novel as a whole, on techniques of narrative now largely abandoned by novelists who have learned their art since the middle of the nineteenth century. It could be shown, I think, that as compared with most of his predecessors, the author of *Tom Jones* had moved a long way in the direction of the imitative and dramatic. Yet it cannot be denied that in many chapters where he might better have "rendered" he merely "states" and that even in the most successful of the scenes in which action and dialogue predominate he leaves far less to inference than we are disposed to like.[12]

Despite all this, however, there are not many novels of comparable length in which the various parts are conceived and developed with a shrewder eye to what is required for a maximum realization of the form.[13] A few examples of this will have to serve, and it is natural to start with the manner in which Fielding handles the incidents that follow directly from Tom's mistakes. The pattern of all of these is much the same: Tom first commits an indiscretion, which is then discovered, and the discovery results in his immediate or eventual embarrassment. Now it is clear that the comic pleasure will be enhanced in proportion as, in each incident, the discovery is made unexpectedly and by precisely those persons whose knowledge of what Tom has done will be most damaging to him, and by as many of these as possible so that the consequences for him are not simple but compounded. Fielding understood this well, and the effects of his understanding are repeatedly evident in *Tom Jones,* from Book IV to the end of the complication. Consider, for example, how he man-

---

[12] Perhaps the chief exception to this, in its relatively large use of "intimation," is the scene of Tom's conversation with Dowling in Book XII, chap. x.

[13] I am indebted for several points in what follows to an unpublished essay by one of my students, Mr. Melvin Seiden.

ages the discovery of Tom's original entanglement with Molly. It is necessary, of course, when Molly is arrested after the fight in the churchyard, that Tom should at once rush to Allworthy with his mistaken confession; but it is not necessary—only highly desirable—that he should intervene in the fight himself as Molly's champion, that Blifil and Square should be with him at the time, that the news of the arrest should reach him while he is dining with Western and Sophia, whose charm he is just beginning to perceive, and that, when he leaves in a hurry, the Squire should joke with his daughter about what he suspects. Or, again, there is the even more complicated and comically disastrous sequence that begins with Tom's drunkenness after Allworthy's recovery. This in itself is ridiculous, since we know the illness has never been serious; but observe how satisfyingly the succeeding embarrassments are made to pile up: Tom's hilarious joy leading to his fight with Blifil; this to his retirement to the grove, his romantic meditation on Sophia, and his surrender to Molly; this to the discovery of his new folly by Blifil and Thwackum; this to the second fight, much bloodier than the first; and this in turn, when the Westerns unexpectedly appear on the scene, to Sophia's fresh discovery of Tom's wildness and, what is much more serious, to the misconstruction of her fainting fit by her aunt, with results that lead presently to the proposal of a match with Blifil, the foolish intervention of Tom, the discovery by Western of the true state of affairs, his angry appeal to Allworthy, Blifil's distorted version of what has happened, Tom's expulsion from home, and Sophia's imprisonment. All this is probable enough, but there is something of the comically wonderful in the educing of so many appropriately extreme consequences from a cause in itself so apparently innocent and trivial. And the same art of making the most out of incidents for the sake of the comic suspense of the plot can be seen at work through the rest of the novel: in the great episode at Upton, for example, where all the happenings are contrived to produce, immediately or remotely, a maximum of pseudo-serious suffering for Tom, and also in the various later scenes in which the discovery to Sophia of Tom's intrigue with her cousin is first narrowly averted, with much embarrassment to him, and then finally made under circumstances that could hardly be worse for the young man. A less accomplished artist seeking to achieve the same general effect through his plot would certainly have missed many of these opportunities.

A less accomplished artist, again, would never have been able to invent or sustain characters so good for the form, as well as so interesting in themselves, as the two Westerns and Partridge. We need not dwell on the multiple uses to which these great humorists are put; it is more important, since the point has been less often discussed, or discussed in part to Fielding's disadvantage, to consider what merits can be found in his handling of the other characters, such as Tom himself, Allworthy, Sophia, and Blifil, who are intended to seem morally sympathetic or antipathetic to us and comically inferior only by virtue of their erroneous acts. With the exception of Sophia, who is made charming and lively enough to constitute in herself good fortune for Tom, they are not endowed with any notably particularized traits, and the question for criticism is whether, given the comic form of the novel as a whole, any more lifelike "doing" would not have entailed a departure from the mean which this imposed. I think the answer is clear for Blifil: he must be made to seem sufficiently formidable in the short run to arouse comic apprehension for Tom but not so formidable as to excite in us active or prolonged feelings of indignation; and any further individualizing of him than we get would almost certainly have upset this balance to the detriment of the whole. The answer is clear also, I think, for Tom. We must consistently favor him against his enemies and think it probable that he should suffer acute embarrassment and remorse when he discovers the consequences of his mistakes; but, on the other hand, any appreciably greater particularizing of his sympathetic traits than is attempted would inevitably have made it difficult for us not to feel his predicaments as seriously as he does himself, and that would have been an error; it is not the least happy of Fielding's inventions, for example, that he repeatedly depicts Tom, especially when he is talking to Sophia or thinking about her, in terms of the clichés of heroic romance. There remains Allworthy, and concerning him the chief doubt arises from a consideration of the important part he is given, along with Sophia, in the definition of Tom's final good fortune. For the purposes of the comic complication it is sufficient that we should see him acting in the character of a severely just magistrate who constantly administers injustice through too great trust in his knowledge of men; it is not for this, however, but for his "amiability" that Tom loves him and cherishes his company in the end; yet of Allworthy's actual possession of that quality we are given few clear signs.

A whole essay, finally, could be written on the masterly way in which Fielding exploited the various devices implicit in his third-person "historical" mode of narration in the service of his comic form. Broadly speaking, his problem was twofold: first, to establish and maintain in the reader a general frame of mind appropriate to the emotional quality of the story as a whole and, second, to make sure that the feelings aroused by his characters at particular moments or stages of the action were kept in proper alignment with the intended over-all effect.

That the first problem is adequately solved there can be little doubt; long before we come to the incidents in which Tom's happiness is put in jeopardy by his own blunders and the malice of Blifil, we have been prepared to expect much unmerited calamity and distress for him, and at the same time to view the prospect without alarm. Our security would doubtless have been less had not Fielding chosen to represent at length the events contained in Books I and II, with the vivid impressions they give of the fallibility of Allworthy on the one hand and of the impotence for permanent harm of the elder Blifil on the other: we cannot but look forward to a repetition of this pattern in the later parts of the novel. This is less important, however, as a determinant of our frame of mind than the guidance given us by the clearly evident attitude of Fielding's narrator. He is, we perceive, a man we can trust, who knows the whole story and still is not deeply concerned; one who understands the difference between good men and bad and who can yet speak with amused indulgence of the first, knowing how prone they are to weakness of intellect, and with urbane scorn, rather than indignation, of the second, knowing that most of them, too, are fools. This combination of sympathetic moral feeling with ironical detachment is bound to influence our expectations from the first, and to the extent that it does so, we tend to anticipate the coming troubles with no more than comic fear.

It is when the troubles come, in Book V and later, that Fielding's second problem emerges; for, given the kinds of things that then happen to Tom and especially the seriousness with which, as a good man, he necessarily takes them, there is always a danger that our original comic detachment may give way, temporarily, to tragicomic feelings of fear, pity, and indignation. That this seldom happens is another sign of how successfully, in *Tom Jones,* the handling of the parts is kept consonant with the formal demands of the whole. It is a question primarily of maximizing the general comic expectations of the reader by minimizing the possible noncomic elements in his inferences about particular situations; and the devices which Fielding uses for the purpose are of several kinds. Sometimes the result is achieved by preventing our attention from concentrating long or closely on potential causes of distress for Tom; it is notable, for example, that we are given no representation of Blifil scheming Tom's ruin before his speech to Allworthy in Book VI, chapter xi, and that from this point until Book XVI Blifil and his intentions are not again brought to the fore. Sometimes the device consists in slurring over a painful scene by generalized narration and then quickly diverting us to an obviously comic sequence in another line of action: this is what Fielding does, to excellent effect, with the incident of Tom's condemnation and banishment; we should feel much more keenly for him if, in the first place, we were allowed to hear more of his talk with Allworthy and, in the second place, were not plunged so soon after into the ridiculous quarrels of the Westerns. Or, again, the expedient may take the simple form of a refusal by the narrator to describe feelings of Tom which, if they were represented directly and at length, might easily excite a noncomic response; as in the accounts of his "madness" at Upton after he finds Sophia's muff and of the torments he endures ("such that even

Thwackum would almost have pitied him") when her message of dismissal comes to him in prison. And the same general minimizing function is also served by the two episodes in the middle part of the novel which have occasioned so much dicussion among Fielding's critics. Both the story told to Tom by the Man of the Hill and that recounted to Sophia by Mrs. Fitzpatrick have plainly the character of elaborate negative analogies to the moral states of the listeners, from which it is possible for the reader to infer, on the eve of the most distressing part of the complication for the hero and heroine, that nothing that may happen to them will be really bad.

These are but a few of the things that can be said, in the light of our general hypothesis about plot, concerning the plot of *Tom Jones* and its relation to the other parts of the novel. They will perhaps suffice to call attention to some aspects of Fielding's constructive art that have commonly been left out of account, from 1749 to the present, even by those who have praised it most highly.

"Fielding" in *Tom Jones*

by Wayne C. Booth

It is frustrating to try to deal critically with such effects [i.e., the functional use of authorial intrusion in fiction], because they can in no way be demonstrated to the reader who has not experienced them. No amount of quotation, no amount of plot summary, can possibly show how fully the implied author's character dominates our reactions to the whole. About all we can do is to look closely at one work, *Tom Jones*, analyzing in static terms what in any successful reading is as sequential and dynamic as the action itself.[1]

Though the dramatized Fielding does serve to pull together many parts of *Tom Jones* that might otherwise seem disconnected, and though he serves dozens of other functions, from the standpoint of strict function he goes too far: much of his commentary relates to nothing but the reader and himself. If we really want to defend the book as art, we must somehow account for these "extraneous" elements. It is not difficult to do so, however, once we think of the effect of our intimacy on our attitude toward the book as a whole. If we read straight through all of the seemingly gratuitous appearances by the narrator, leaving out the story of Tom, we discover a running account of growing intimacy between the narrator and the reader, an account with a kind of plot of its own and a separate denouement. In the prefatory chapter to his final volume, the narrator makes this denouement explicit, suggesting a distinct interest in the "story" of his relationship with the reader. This interest certainly requires some explanation if we wish to claim that *Tom Jones* is a unified work of art and not half-novel, half-essay.

> We are now, reader, arrived at the last stage of our long journey. As we have, therefore, travelled together through so many pages, let us behave to one another like fellow-travellers in a stagecoach, who have passed several days in the company of each other; and who, notwithstanding any bicker-

[1] Perhaps the best defense of Fielding's commentary is that of A. D. McKillop, in *Early Masters of English Fiction* (Lawrence, Kan., 1956), esp. p. 123.

ings or little animosities which may have occurred on the road, generally make all up at last, and mount, for the last time, into their vehicle with cheerfulness and good-humour.

The farewell goes on for several paragraphs, and at times the bantering tone of much of the work is entirely abandoned. "And now, my friend, I take this opportunity (as I shall have no other) of heartily wishing thee well. If I have been an entertaining companion to thee, I promise thee it is what I have desired. If in anything I have offended, it was really without any intention."

It may be extravagant to use the term "subplot" for the story of our relationship with this narrator. Certainly the narrator's "life" and Tom Jones's life are much less closely parallel than we expect in most plots and subplots. In *Lear,* Gloucester's fate parallels and reinforces Lear's. In *Tom Jones,* the "plot" of our relationship with Fielding-as-narrator has no similarity to the story of Tom. There is no complication, not even any sequence except for the gradually increasing familiarity and intimacy leading to farewell. And much of what we admire or enjoy in the narrator is in most respects quite different from what we like or enjoy in his hero.

Yet somehow a genuine harmony of the two dramatized elements is produced. It is from the narrator's norms that Tom departs when he gets himself into trouble, yet Tom is always in harmony with his most important norms. Not only does he reassure us constantly that Tom's heart is always in the right place, his presence reassures us of both the moral and the literary rightness of Tom's existence. As we move through the novel under his guidance, watching Tom sink to the depths, losing, as it appears, Allworthy's protection, Sophia's love, and his own shaky hold on decency, we experience for him what R. S. Crane has called the "comic analogue of fear." [2] And our growing intimacy with Fielding's dramatic version of himself produces a kind of comic analogue of the true believer's reliance on a benign providence in real life. It is not just that he promises a happy ending. In a fictional world that offers no single character who is both wise and good—even Allworthy, though all worthy, is no model of perspicacity—the author is always there on his platform to remind us, through his wisdom and benevolence, of what human life ought to be and might be. What is more, his self-portrait is of a life enriched by a vast knowledge of literary culture and of a mind of great creative power—qualities which could never be so fully conveyed through simply exercising them without comment on the dramatic materials of Tom's story.

For the reader who becomes too much aware of the author's claim to superlative virtues, the effect may fail. He may seem merely to be posing.

[2] *Critics and Criticism,* ed. R. S. Crane (Chicago, 1952), p. 637. [See p. 68 of this volume.]

For the reader with his mind on the main business, however, the narrator becomes a rich and provocative chorus. It is his wisdom and learning and benevolence that permeate the world of the book, set its comic tone between the extremes of sentimental indulgence and scornful indignation, and in a sense redeem Tom's world of hypocrites and fools.

One can imagine, perhaps, a higher standard of virtue, wisdom, or learning than the narrator's. But for most of us he succeeds in being the highest possible in his world—and, at least for the nonce, in ours. He is not trying to write for any other world, but for *this* one he strikes the precise medium between too much and too little piety, benevolence, learning, and worldly wisdom.[3] When he draws to the end of his farewell, then, at a time when we know we are to lose him, and uses terms which inevitably move us across the barrier to death itself, we find, lying beneath our amusement at his playful mode of farewell, something of the same feeling we have when we lose a close friend, a friend who has given us a gift which we can never repay. The gift he leaves—his book—is himself, precisely himself. The author has created this self as he has written the book. The book and the friend are one. "For however short the period may be of my own performances, they will most probably outlive their own infirm author, and the weakly productions of his abusive contemporaries." Was Fielding literally infirm as he wrote that sentence? It matters not in the least. It is not Fielding we care about, but the narrator created to speak in his name.

[3] *Ibid.*, p. 652. William Empson gives a lively and convincing defense of Fielding's code and of the moral stature of *Tom Jones* in *"Tom Jones," Kenyon Review*, XX (Spring, 1958), 217–49. [See pp. 33–55 of this volume.] Though Empson mars his case a bit by arriving "circuitously at what Fielding tells us plainly enough" (C. J. Rawson, "Professor Empson's *Tom Jones*," *Notes and Queries*, N.S., VI [November, 1959], 400), his statement is a valuable antidote to the oversimplifications which have been used in dismissing Fielding and his commentary.

Fielding and the Uses of Style

by Robert Alter

When Fielding, in both the Preface to *Joseph Andrews* and in the prefatory chapters of *Tom Jones*, speaks of the genre he is inventing as a comic variant of the Homeric epic, the core of serious truth in his critical stricture is qualified by irony; the reader is offered excellent guidance which he must follow with caution because of a lurking suspicion that the deft hand of the narrator, in the midst of explanatory gestures, is somehow pulling his leg. The very presence of such prefaces, to begin with, should serve to remind us that Fielding is the first of the great intellectual novelists: like Flaubert, James, Joyce, Gide, he is anxious to define the novel in terms of literary tradition, modern and classical, and, like them, he theorizes about what he writes as he writes it. Fielding's association of the novel with the epic is suggestive in several ways, but what is most relevant here are the implied assumptions about the function of language and the relationship of the writer to his audience.

A good deal has been said in recent years about the novel as private experience: the living-out of fantasy, which is of course essentially private, is usually thought of as the characteristic act of novel-reading. But this surely does not account for our total experience as readers of novels, and Fielding, with a neoclassical conception of the epic very much in mind, repeatedly insists that a novel is something to be shared by a community of the discriminating. The force of the very first sentence in *Tom Jones*, which introduces the metaphor of the feast that will be sustained throughout the novel, is to make clear at once that the novel is conceived as public experience: "An author ought to consider himself, not as a gentleman who gives a private or eleemosynary treat, but rather as one who keeps a public ordinary, at which all persons are welcome for their money."

Now, the most public aspect of a literary work is its language, for words we all share in common, while the kinds of imaginings to which words stir us inevitably take place in the privacy of the individual mind.

"Fielding and the Uses of Style" by Robert Alter. *From* Novel: A Forum on Fiction, *I (Fall, 1967), 53–63. Copyright © 1967 by Robert Alter. Reprinted by permission of the author and publisher.*

And it seems to me that the most fundamental influence of the epic on Fielding is in his decision to base the novel on the artfully ostentatious manipulation of words. In keeping with the general function of rhythmic beat, extended simile, and formulaic recurrence in the epic, his most essential procedure as a novelist is constantly to enrich his fictional world by reminding us in different ways of the literary artifice through which that world comes into being. The most obtrusive expressions of this tendency in his writing are, of course, his parodies of epic devices. Most of these, though ingenious enough, are far from representing an imaginative assimilation of the epic: the great mock-epic set-pieces, like Molly Seagrim's churchyard brawl or Joseph Andrews' battle with the hunting dogs, are brilliant entertainments, not novelistic revelations. Of much more significance to Fielding's achievement as a creator of the novel is his success in fashioning a stylized language which, through the fine control of tone, rhythm, imagery, syntax, by the shrewd play with and against the received meanings of words, achieves the qualities of precision of reference, complexity of statement, esthetically pleasing form, that are traditionally associated with the language of poetry.

Reading Fielding, and even more, rereading Fielding, we are repeatedly made aware of the way he maneuvers us into seeing characters, actions, values, society at large, from exactly the angle of vision he wants. The famous moment in *Tom Jones* when the philosopher Square is discovered behind the arras in Molly Seagrim's bedroom offers a kind of paradigm for Fielding's general method. The rug nailed over Molly's makeshift closet falls just as she is berating Tom for his infidelity, and the contents of the closet are suddenly revealed:

> . . . *where among other female utensils appeared (with shame I write it, and with sorrow will it be read)—the philosopher Square, in a posture (for the place would not near admit his standing upright) as ridiculous as can possibly be conceived.*
>
> *The posture, indeed, in which he stood was not greatly unlike that of a soldier who is tied neck and heels; or rather resembling the attitude in which we often see fellows in the public streets of London, who are not suffering but deserving punishment by so standing. (V,5)*

The phrase here that has often, and understandably, evoked comment is, of course, "among other female utensils." It is a miracle of satiric compression: the addition of that lethal "other" places Square for us precisely where Fielding wants him, reducing the teacher of noble ethical ideals to a kind of ambulatory dildo, heaped together with sundry unnamed female appurtenances which, as Molly's intimate possessions, would in all likelihood be neither very clean nor sweet nor pleasant to behold. The satiric point of the phrase, moreover, transfixes Molly together with Square, because the application here of "female utensils" brilliantly exposes the crude standard of sexual utilitarianism upon which she bases her relationships with men, Tom included. Having demolished his target, Fielding now circles back upon it with a more rhetorically oblique method of attack. The narration pauses for a moment over the contorted posture of the philosopher—a man whose name and motto of "right rule of reason" imply geometrical rectitude—and then goes on to offer two detailed similes, ostensibly in order to help us visualize his awkward position. But their real function, clearly, is to contaminate the already exposed image of Square through association with scurrilous objects of comparison: and so his posture is likened to that of a trussed-up soldier being punished for moral dereliction, and to the shameless squat of the London rabble in the act of using the streets as a privy. Throughout Fielding, similes are employed in a similar way, not merely as parodies of the extended epic simile, but as instruments to wrest from us, through the pressure of rhetorical persistence, a kind of comic assent to the writer's satiric judgments. With the most elaborate mock-solemnity, lawyers are carefully compared to butchers and hangmen, gossips to dove-rending kites, mercenary fathers of marriageable daughters to heartless bawds selling maidenheads to the highest bidder, and so forth.

145496

The passage we have been considering illustrates one aspect of Fielding's prose which needs more emphasis than it has generally received. Because of the various prefatory materials, the constant authorial asides, the leisurely elaboration of figures of speech, one naturally thinks of Fielding as an expansive writer; but there is a systole as well as a diastole in the movement of his prose, and his apparently easy manner can arrive suddenly at the most remarkable concentration of expression. When, for example, he comments in *Joseph Andrews* on the surprisingly gracious reception of Pamela by Lady Booby, his explanation is a complete essay in social criticism in twelve innocent-looking words: "for she was perfectly polite, nor had any vice inconsistent with good-breeding" (IV,4). One can see at such moments why the conventional distinction between essayistic and novelistic passages in Fielding's fiction is essentially false. The social criticism here has resonance because it reverberates against the actions and passions of Lady Booby, whom we have seen in all her towering sexual egotism and relentless sexual hypocrisy both as a realized character and as the representative of a particular social code. Presentation of character and social commentary are so entrammeled together that it would be foolish to try to separate them. There is, moreover, no real difference in kind between this concise observation on the morals of Lady Booby and the longer "digressions" in Fielding. The point is that the moral and social commentator, Fielding the so-called essayist, is *always* present: often he makes his presence felt, as here, by the briefest passing reflection, or by the mere choice of an adjective or the position of a verb; at times he moves gracefully through long and elaborate comic glissades from the particular to the universal and back again; but the narrative is everywhere one weave, steadily editorializing, sometimes conspicuously, sometimes inobtrusively.

It is of course the inobtrusiveness that needs to be observed. Fielding himself warns us in *Tom Jones* that the reader must be constantly on the alert if he is to read the novel with pleasure and profit: "we shall not indulge thy laziness where nothing but thy own attention is required; for thou art highly mistaken if thou dost imagine that we intended, when we began this great work, to leave thy sagacity nothing to do" (XI,9). As in a proper reading of Pope's couplets, a prehensile activity of the mind is called for, not only to seize on slippery hints about characters and plot and the application of veiled allusions, but also to catch the quick thrust of satirical wit in a phrase whose suddenness or obliquity scarcely gives us opportunity to take in its pointed meaning. It is easy for a reader to sail right past the epigram on Lady Booby without seeing the scarifying flash of its satire, or to miss, through sheer swiftness, the sharply ironic contradiction of the phrases that describe how the falsely accused Partridge "left the country, where he was in danger of starving, with the universal compassion of all his neighbours" (*TJ*,II,6).

The reader is also frequently required to attend not only to what words say but to how they are arranged if he is to perceive their latent meaning. The main point, for example, in Fielding's report of the demise of Sir Thomas Booby is communicated through a finesse of syntax: "At this time, an accident happened which put a stop to those agreeable walks [of Joseph's and Lady Booby's], which probably would have soon puffed up the cheeks of Fame, and caused her to blow her brazen trumpet through the town; and this was no other than the death of Sir Thomas Booby, who, departing this life, left his disconsolate lady confined to her house, as closely as if she herself had been attacked by some violent disease" (*JA*,I,5). The sentence nicely illustrates why, from Fielding's point of view, there are better things to be done with language than to go poking around in people's minds. The finely controlled movement of revelation and the facetiously orotund use of stock allegory are obviously the work of a self-conscious omniscient narrator; yet the sentence, without actually imitating the processes of Lady Booby's consciousness, does mirror in its formal arrangement the distorted pattern of her values. The first mention of that regrettable accident, death, is almost buried under a series of introductory clauses, which, appropriately, are mainly devoted to Lady Booby's reputation; and then the sentence moves on at once to the lamentable confinement of the new widow, sliding through Sir Thomas' death in a mere participial phrase and thus reducing it—as indeed it is reduced in Lady Booby's perspective of polite self-centeredness—to a kind of social inadvertency: the husband leaves his lady, "departing this life," as a man might be described forgetting his hat.

This prehensile activity of the mind is most especially and continually required for the reader to seize upon Fielding's coy ironies in the abundant variety of their disguises. It is, moreover, through his use of irony that Fielding most effectively focuses the moral meanings of his fiction by directing our attention to his language. Language, as Fielding understands it and works with it, is both the necessary instrument for moral analysis and one of the principal means through which we justify our institutionalized hypocrisies, deceive others and ourselves as well. His most typical procedure is to order a statement so that awareness of its ironic counter-meaning gradually dawns on us, throwing a retrospective light on key words or phrases and illuminating the falseness of their conventional application: we read forward to find out what is happening, and, so to speak, backward, re-examining the tools of communication that belong to both the literary medium and our own moral world. Thus Fielding explains why Dr. Blifil, who has the misfortune to be married, does not even think of "criminal indulgences" with Bridget Allworthy: "This was owing either to his religion, as is most probable, or to the purity of his passion, which was fixed on those things which matrimony only, and not criminal correspondence, could put him in possession of, or could give him any title to" (I,10). By the time we arrive at the double insistence on the rights of property at the end, we realize that "purity" has been used in a chemical, not a moral, sense—that is, unadulterated, suffering no admixture—and, as the mock-morality of Dr. Blifil's motives is laid bare, we begin to wonder whether marriage for gain as he coldly conceives it might not be the most "criminal correspondence" of all. Certainly, Bridget's liaison with the young Summer, about which we learn much later, seems innocent by comparison.

On the level of style, irony operates on the reader not only to make him aware of mutually qualifying meanings, but also to implicate him in a particular relationship with the narrator and the material narrated. This relationship is important in winning both his assent to values affirmed through the novel and his sympathy for the kind of literary enterprise that is being undertaken. Irony, as we are often reminded, implies both complicity and superiority—complicity between the ironist and the discerner of the irony, who share a sense of intelligent superiority to its unwitting objects, or to any hypothetical persons who would take it at face value. The ironic attitude boosts Fielding, and his readers with him, to a firm position of elevation over the world he describes, and while few writers since have wanted to rise to such Olympian heights, some of the greatest novelists—Cervantes, Jane Austen, Flaubert, Joyce— have resembled Fielding in maintaining a careful ironic distance be-

tween themselves and the life they recorded. The perspective of irony
is invaluable because of a danger inherent in the basic impulse of the
novel to immerse us in contemporary reality; for reality seen from so
close is likely to be a shapeless mass of clamorous particulars which can
easily subvert both moral intelligence and esthetic lucidity. This is clearly
one basis for Fielding's objection to the whole method of *Pamela,* for his
repeated insistence, *contra* Richardson, that a novelist must exercise the
highest degree of selectivity and the finest narrative tact.

Irony, then, is used by the narrators of *Joseph Andrews* and *Tom
Jones* to establish for the reader an attitude toward the worlds of those
novels which is both minutely attentive and coolly withdrawn. Fielding
embraces the contemporary world with the delight of one who has re-
created it lovingly, and yet his view of it remains oddly concessive—just
as he is concessive in using the formula "in vulgar language" or "in plain
English" when he begins, grudgingly, to translate one of his high-flying
periphrases into the ordinary speech of mere groundlings. Because
through irony Fielding can simultaneously engage the world of immediate experience and imply its moral and esthetic inadequacy, his irony
is inseparable from the meticulously preserved decorum of his style: they
work together to control with nice precision how we are to think and feel
about his fictional events. The quality of archness that characterizes so
many of his statements is especially relevant here. Though his sly ingenuity may occasionally seem a bit self-admiring, it almost always has
the effect of affirming an underlying moral-esthetic viewpoint, as, for example, in his ambiguous account of Bridget Allworthy's attraction to
Captain Blifil:

> *Though Miss Bridget was a woman of the greatest delicacy of taste, yet
> such were the charms of the captain's conversation, that she totally over-
> looked the defects of his person. She imagined, and perhaps very wisely,
> that she should enjoy more agreeable minutes with the captain than with
> a much prettier fellow; and forewent the consideration of pleasing her
> eyes, in order to procure herself much more solid satisfaction. (I,11)*

The way the passage turns back upon itself ironically is clear: when
we come to the final procurement of "solid satisfaction," our hovering
suspicion about earlier phrases is fully confirmed; we realize that "delicacy" has been used in its older sense of "addiction to sensuous pleasures," that the captain's conversation is carnal, not verbal (as in the
frequent eighteenth-century usage, "criminal conversation"), and that
Bridget's enjoyment with the captain is a matter of "agreeable minutes"
rather than hours because of the physiological limitations of a certain
universal human activity, too well-known to be mentioned. Fielding goes
on to supply a corresponding sexual innuendo for Captain Blifil's view
of his obligations to Bridget, and later (II,2), in order to assure us that

we have not mistaken his meaning, he announces that "by reason of a fright" Bridget gave birth to a son eight months after the marriage ceremony.

It is worth considering for a moment what Fielding gains by reporting this relationship in such an archly oblique manner. It is obvious that other methods of narration here might be far more vivid and dramatic. A writer in the naturalist tradition could give us Bridget's quickened breath and sweaty palms, the grotesque coquetry of her amorous leer, the way she would sidle up to the captain, brushing her heavy flesh against him, and, finally, the two aging, graceless bodies shuddering together in furtive pleasure. Or, a novelist interested in rendering consciousness would reproduce Bridget's mental excitement, her kinesthetic response to the potent maleness of Captain Blifil's presence, catching us up in the tide of eagerness after frustration of a spinster who has tasted pleasure once, but, since the death of her lover over a year earlier, has been forced to live in arid celibacy. But a reader with such expectations, as Fielding dryly observes in justifying the omission of details about those most "ordinary occurrences" between Tom and Lady Bellaston, "is one whose devotion to the fair sex, like that of the Papists to their saints, wants to be raised by the help of pictures" (XIII,9). Fielding's decorous reticence is clearly not the result of any personal inclination to prudery—we need only recall in this connection his hilarious allusions in *Shamela* to the size, function, and vulnerability of the sexual organs. On the contrary, the attitude communicated through his oblique manner is a sly knowingness about sexual matters. You and I, the narrator suggests to us through his irony and his stylistic decorum, are both men of the world who know what it's all about and who certainly understand what a frustrated spinster is really after; but we are, after all, cultured people who should therefore observe the proprieties of literature; we can apprehend the world and judge it without descending in our discourse to the level of its acts and words. The moral facts of real life, however sordid, are recognized and encompassed—and, of course, made immensely amusing—by this method of presentation, while the unseemly rawness of experience is carefully distanced: we are invited to infer its pungency without directly tasting it.

Paradoxically, Fielding's decision to avoid the grossness of exhaustive realism generates in his novels another kind of realism, which is essentially social and moral in nature. To bring us any closer to the undercover activities of Bridget and her lusty captain would be to take advantage of the special literary privilege of voyeurism, which, admittedly, is a favorite perspective of novelists from Richardson on. Fielding, however, is not at all interested in the affective side of the lovers' relationship but rather in what it reveals about the nature of man, conceived in Augustan terms morally not psychologically, living in society. We discover the fact of Bridget's premarital indulgence much the way we would if we really lived in the community to which she belongs—through a process of alert inference, initiated by a predisposition to suspicion to which Fielding's prose has rhetorically conditioned us, just as society morally conditions its members to cast a cold eye of suspicion on one another. Baldly stated, Bridget's carnal weakness would be a mere crudity or an uninteresting commonplace; but as Fielding makes us infer it, the bare fact hides teasingly behind a veil of innuendo, and innuendo of course implies attitude, bearing with it a sort of hovering moral judgment, potentially emphatic, yet not quite proper to be expressed. The realism of this whole procedure, it should be stressed, is not in any "reproduction" of reality but in the creation through language of a process both analogous and esthetically superior to one we live out in reality: we pick up Fielding's innuendo through the discrimination of verbal ambiguities in a beautifully wrought stylistic structure, not from the knowing smirk and tattletale whisper of gossip.

One briefer example should show still more clearly how authorial archness and stylistic decorum are manipulated to place us in just the relation to the novel that the writer wants. At two points in *Tom Jones*, Fielding introduces a discreet but strategic hint that, while Tom is out in the bushes tumbling his wench, young Blifil may be off in the woodshed, gratifying his desires with the aid of his own right hand: "The charms of Sophia had not made the least impression on Blifil; not that his heart was pre-engaged; neither was he totally insensible of beauty, or had any aversion to women; but his appetites were by nature so moderate, that he was able, by philosophy, or by study, or by some other method, easily to subdue them" (VI,4, and compare X,9, last paragraph). Fielding's concessive realism is brilliantly effective here. Unlike Joyce, who could make out of the poetic description of an act of onanism one of the tours de force of the modern novel, Fielding has esthetic misgivings as to whether this kind of reality belongs in serious literature. But from his perspective of moral realist, he squarely accepts it as a common human act we all know about and therefore as a distinctly possible act in the world of his novel. By merely hinting at it, however, with such sly indirection, he implicates us in his assumptions of taste and morals and casts over Blifil a darkening shadow of innuendo; what is communicated is not the "objective fact" that Blifil masturbates, but the powerful suspicion that he does, accompanied by the feeling, "Yes, and what a sneaking, mean-spirited, dirty little act it is!"

From all this, it ought to be apparent why in *Joseph Andrews* and, to a much greater degree, in *Tom Jones,* Fielding uses a self-dramatizing narrator who in a sense is, as some readers have suggested, his most fully realized character. Since his whole literary method works on the tacit assumption of a community of values, both moral and esthetic, between

writer and reader—like that which united the epic poet and his audience
—it is logical that he should reinforce this shared outlook by speaking
through a witty, humane *persona* with whom we can feel a sort of urbane
camaraderie. Or perhaps it might be more precise to say that he creates
rather than reinforces shared outlooks, for Fielding is clearly aware that
in his age the community of values, like the community of men, has
lost much of the intactness it may once have had—this is, from one point
of view, why he must write comic-epic novels and not serious epic poems.
He proceeds in his novels not only by affirming accepted values but also,
as we have seen, by qualifying or even redefining some of them, as he
redefines in *Tom Jones* the whole traditional literary idea of the hero.
Through the creation of a narrator whom we come to like and trust, he
is able to conjure up a sense of common viewpoint with the reader that
is part actual persuasion, part fictional equivalent of real agreement. His
success in this effort is one reason why so little in his two comic novels
has dated despite all the obvious and intricate ways in which his writing
is anchored in his period. We may no longer all think of masturbation as
the unmitigated nastiness Fielding must have assumed his readers would
judge it to be, but that hardly matters: the rhetorical strategy through
which he suggests Blifil's manner of satisfying his "passion" makes us
concur in the narrator's view of the act with an eager sympathy that is
more than the willing suspension of disbelief.

One can also see from such examples that the whole world of Fielding's novels, and not merely the language, is carefully stylized. He was
not only following epic precedents, in this respect, but was applying
techniques learned in his years of writing for the theater. For obvious
reasons, speech and action invented for the stage, especially the comic
stage, tend to be heightened or exaggerated representations of reality,
so contrived that the characteristic lines are sharper, more immediately
self-revealing, than they could be in actual experience. Much of the action in both *Joseph Andrews* and *Tom Jones* has this quality of stylization, cutting contours that are manifestly bolder than life. A whole series
of broadly comic actions comes to mind—the climactic chain of bedroom
confusions at Lady Booby's in *Joseph Andrews*, the wild free-for-all at
the Upton inn in *Tom Jones*, Squire Western's precipitous change from
the chase for Sophia to a chase for a fox. Less obvious are the many small
actions that, on examination, read like comic stage directions translated
into the idiom of the novel—Beau Didapper, after sheathing his hanger
at the end of an averted brawl with Joseph, taking out a pocket-glass to
re-adjust his hair (*JA*,IV,11); Honour, rhapsodizing about Jones and
oblivious to her mistress' blushes because she is all the while mesmerized
by her own features in a mirror (*TJ*,IV,14).

Fielding's dialogue is just as pervasively stylized. This is apparent in
the language his characters speak, which shifts from self-parody to literary

parody to formal comic soliloquy, and even when simulating the vividness of earthy speech, is an artful exaggeration rather than a transcription of it. Equally important, what the characters say as well as how they say it is usually stylized; much of it is rather improbable by the standards of ordinary realism but comically revealing and perfectly right in context. Thus Lady Booby offers an impassioned plea for the impregnability of her virtue: " 'If I had ever discovered any wantonness, any lightness in my behaviour: if I had followed the example of some whom thou hast, I believe, seen, in allowing myself indecent liberties, even with a husband; but the dear man who is gone' (*here she began to sob*), 'was he alive again (*then she produced tears*), 'could not upbraid me with any one act of tenderness or passion' " (IV,6). In real life, of course, a wife who despised her husband and lusted after a serving-boy would never say this; Lady Booby's hypocrisy confesses itself with such splendidly lucid theatricality that it is entirely appropriate for Fielding to include actual stage-directions, properly italicized.

Or again, Mrs. Deborah Wilkins' charitable comments on the infant Tom are what not the sharpest-tongued spinster, though her soul were as shriveled as a prune, could have actually said, but precisely because of their bold stylization, they provide a wonderful moment of comic illumination:

> It goes against me to touch these misbegotten wretches, whom I don't look upon as my fellow-creatures. Faugh! how it stinks! It doth not smell like a Christian. If I might be so bold to give my advice, I would have it put in a basket, and sent out and laid at the church-warden's door. It is a good night, only a little rainy and windy; and if it was well wrapt up, and put in a warm basket, it is two to one but it lives till it is found in the morning. (*I,3*)

There is, to be sure, a significant difference between stylization and mere exaggeration, but I am convinced that in all these aspects of Fielding's writing the category of stylization is properly applicable because in all of them one can discern the essential element of *formal design,* which at once attests to the shaping hand of the craftsman and, however partially, suggests the unifying conception of meaning and manner that underlies the whole work. The design is more beautifully and firmly elaborated in *Tom Jones* than in *Joseph Andrews,* though it is largely present in the earlier novel as well. Perhaps the most exhilarating experience in reading *Tom Jones*—especially for us in an age when so many unities are shattered, so many styles of art and life deliberately fragmented—is the sense communicated through the poised arabesques of style of a magisterial intelligence, supremely in command of the whole world it presents us. In Fielding, as in his great admirer, Gibbon, the periodic style serves as a kind of immanent metaphor of control, continually demonstrating the writer's ability to hold the varied data of a multifaceted reality in coherent and significant order. His periods, ironically eloquent and eloquently ironic, are often small replicas of the architectural form of the whole novel. Dorothy Van Ghent has aptly noted this particular effect of mirrored patterns: while discussing the complicated unity of structure of *Tom Jones,* she observes incidentally that "many of Fielding's sentences are complex little 'plots' in themselves, where the reader must follow a suspended subject through a functional ornament of complications—qualifying dependent clauses and prepositional phrases and eloquent pauses—to the dramatic predication or denouement."

Such intricately developed periodic sentences are paradigmatic, but not quite typical, of the repetition of pattern, or design, in *Tom Jones,* since the varied demands of a long narrative often require more constricted, less elaborate syntactical structures. What I think lies at the heart of the pattern in Fielding's prose, what constitutes the recurrent element which works almost subliminally to remind us that everything in the novel has the integrity of an artifact, is his endlessly varied reduction of so many of his materials to sharply antithetical structures whose members are held in tight balance against each other. Perhaps, if we were determined enough at psychological or moral conjecture, we could assign an explicit "meaning" to this design of balance, but it seems wiser to conclude simply that it is a bedrock of esthetic preference for Fielding. Like many novelists after him, his esthetic assumptions and his habits of patterning language seem to have been crucially influenced by the kind of poetry he admired, and the English poet *par excellence* for him was, inevitably, Alexander Pope. No one else who has written English could have demonstrated to Fielding so spectacularly the beauties of finely controlled, elastically varied balancing, or the power of sudden, searing illumination generated by sharp antithesis.

Because Fielding does not write under the high compression of heroic couplets, the wit of his antitheses never detonates so sharply or rapidly as that of Pope's sustained volleys. Nevertheless, I suspect he owes at least partly to his reading of Pope the predilection for balancing his statements in neat see-saw movements that raise mere contrasts to strict causal relationships where, by a law of comic physics, one side must go up if the other goes down. This, for example, is the way he compares Squire Western and his sister: "as the brother never foresaw anything at a distance, but was most sagacious in immediately seeing everything the moment it happened; so the sister eternally foresaw at a distance, but was not so quick-sighted to objects before her eyes . . . and, indeed, both their several talents were excessive; for, as the sister often foresaw what never came to pass, so the brother often saw much more than was actually the truth" (X,8). Fielding's fondness for neatly antithetical pairs of characters has often been noted, and the two Westerns are of course just such a pair; but the degree to which the same kind of antithesis shapes his whole style has not, I think, been sufficiently observed. It is the matrix of his prose not only at obvious moments like this one, when two characters are being compared, but also very often when the actions of a single character are reported.

Thus Fielding offers to explain why Mrs. Wilkins, after taking so much time to fix her hair upon receiving a midnight summons from Mr. Allworthy, is so terrified at the sight of him in his night-shirt: "It will not be wondered at that a creature who had so strict a regard to decency in her own person should be shocked at the least deviation from it in another" (I,3). The concise antithesis both produces a witty neatness of formulation and teases us into thought. Mrs. Wilkins' two unrelated actions, one a result of her vanity, the other of her prudery, are bracketed together by rhetoric and set into see-saw motion on a fulcrum of specious causal logic. Or perhaps, we begin to wonder, the two actions are related, though not in the way the sentence pretends: Mrs. Wilkins before the mirror could conceivably have had vague expectations from being called at that hour to her master's bedroom which she would scarcely admit to herself, and her excessive shock at his dishabille might be a spinster's fears of what she unconsciously anticipates, or possibly, the result of a resolution to yield herself while preserving her reputation for virtue through the shrillest protestations of concern for it.

From instances like these, one can see that Fielding belongs with the group of novelists which includes such varied figures as Sterne, Conrad, Proust, Joyce, and Faulkner, for whom style is not just the means of conveying or framing events but, often, the event itself. In this respect, the recent film version of *Tom Jones* was faithful to the original in using black-and-white footage and comic subtitles at the beginning, in occasionally projecting a still shot, and in other ways making the manipulation of the medium itself generate some of the comedy. At times Fielding seems almost to anticipate such cinematic techniques, as in his description of the duel between Tom and Fitzpatrick: "Jones . . . pressed on so boldly upon Fitzpatrick, that he beat down his guard, and sheathed one half of his sword in the body of the said gentleman, who had no sooner received it than he stepped backwards, dropped the point of his sword, and leaning upon it, cried, 'I have satisfaction enough: I am a dead man'" (XVI,10). The action itself here is not necessarily funny but the manner of its relation is hilarious. With a superb sense of comic timing, Fielding speeds up the pace of narration, much the way reducing the number of frames in filming turns natural movements into ridiculous staccato jerks, and so we have Fitzpatrick, "the said gentleman," suddenly impaled on a sword, confessing, before we can quite finish blinking, that he has had satisfaction enough.

Moments such as this, however, are simply bright comic byplay. What is, finally, the most important function of Fielding's style, with its recurrence of antitheses and syntactical couplings, is the continually integrating activity brought about through it. Pretense is related to practice, one character to another, one act or posture to another which follows or to one in a completely different sphere of experience, the habits of the upper classes to those of the lower, country custom to city fashion, what goes on in England to the general state of the supposedly Christian nations. An intriguing aspect of the novel as a genre is that it has been driven from its inception by two opposite impulses—to explore the nature of private experience, which had been given a new and problematic importance by the changing social order, and to imagine the whole sweep of contemporary society, in a period when that was becoming progressively less imaginable. Fielding clearly belongs with those novelists who seek to evoke panorama, moral as well as social; he is attracted to the epic, in fact, partly because of its striking panoramic aspects, as Parson Adams' glowing praise of *opsis* in Homer (*JA*,III,2) attests. But since Fielding's plots obviously represent a relatively limited selection of social possibilities and moral situations, it is chiefly through his integrating style that he achieves the artistic illusion of an all-encompassing vision of contemporary life.

Chronology of Important Dates

Fielding's Life

1707 April 22: Fielding born at Sharpham Park, near Glastonbury, Somerset.

1711

1714

1715–16

1719–24 Education at Eton.

1721

1726

1727

1728 January 29: his first work published—*The Masquerade,* a satiric poem. February 16: his first play produced—*Love in Several Masques.* March 16: registers as student of letters, University of Leyden.

1729 August: discontinues studies at Leyden. Autumn: takes up residence in London.

1730–37 His career as a dramatist. During this period his plays —all of them comedies—included *The Author's Farce* (1730), *Rape upon Rape* (1730), *Tom Thumb* (1730), *The Modern Husband* (1732), *The Miser* (1733), *Don Quixote in England* (1734), *Pasquin* (1736), *The Historical Register* (1737).

The Age

May: Pope's *Essay on Criticism.*

August: death of Queen Anne and accession of George I.

September–February: Jacobite Rebellion.

April, 1719: Defoe's *Robinson Crusoe.*

Sir Robert Walpole begins his twenty-year tenure as Prime Minister.

October: Swift's *Gulliver's Travels.*

June: death of George I and accession of George II.

January: Gay's *Beggar's Opera.*
May: Pope's *Dunciad* in three books.

	Fielding's Life	*The Age*
1731		April: death of Defoe.
1732		December: death of Gay.
1733–34		February–January: Pope's *Essay on Man*.
1734	November 28: elopement and marriage with Charlotte Cradock.	
1737	November 1: begins study of law at the Middle Temple.	June: passage of the Theatrical Licensing Act.
1739	November 15–June, 1741: edits *The Champion*.	October: war with Spain.
1740	June 20: called to the bar.	November: Richardson's *Pamela*.
1741	April 4: *Shamela*.	
1742	February 22: *Joseph Andrews*.	February: Walpole resigns. March: Pope's *New Dunciad*.
1743	April 12: *Miscellanies*, including *Jonathan Wild* and *A Journey from This World to the Next*.	
1744	November: death of his wife.	March: war with France. May: death of Pope. December: formation of "Broad-Bottom" Administration.
1745	October: pamphlets supporting the Hanoverian government against the Jacobites— *A Serious Address to the People of Great Britain, The History of the Present Rebellion*, and *A Dialogue between the Devil, the Pope, and the Pretender*.	October: death of Swift.
1745–46	November 5–June 17, 1746: edits *The True Patriot*.	August–April 16: Jacobite Rebellion, under the Young Pretender, Charles Edward Stuart.
1747	November 27: marries Mary Daniel. December 5–November 5, 1748: edits *The Jacobite's Journal*.	December–December, 1748: Richardson's *Clarissa*.

Fielding's Life	*The Age*
1748	March 28–June 2: manages puppet theater under name of "Mme. de la Nash." October 15: writes to Richardson praising *Clarissa*. October 25: final writ empowering him to act as magistrate for district of Westminster, London.	January: Smollett's *Roderick Random.* October: Treaty of Aix-la-Chapelle, ending war with France.
1749	January: commissioned magistrate for County of Middlesex. February 3–10: *Tom Jones.*	
1751	January: *Enquiry into the Causes of the Late Increase of Robbers.* December 19: *Amelia.*	February: Smollett's *Peregrine Pickle.*
1752	January 4–November 25: *The Covent-Garden Journal.*	
1753	January: *Proposal for Making an Effectual Provision for the Poor.* Autumn–winter: successfully executes plan for suppressing crime in London.	November–March, 1754: Richardson's *Sir Charles Grandison.*
1754	April: seriously ill, he resigns from the magistracy. June 26–August 7: his voyage to Lisbon, the *Journal* of which was posthumously published in 1755. October 8: his death in Junqueira near Lisbon.	

Notes on the Editor and Contributors

MARTIN C. BATTESTIN (b. 1930), editor of this anthology, is Professor of English at the University of Virginia. He is the author of *The Moral Basis of Fielding's Art* (1959) and of several articles on Fielding. Having edited *Joseph Andrews* both for the Riverside series (1961) and for the definitive Wesleyan Edition of Fielding's Works (1967), he is at present preparing editions of *Tom Jones* and *Amelia*.

ROBERT ALTER (b. 1935) is Associate Professor of Comparative Literature at the University of California, Berkeley. He has written *Rogue's Progress* (1964) and has recently completed a study of Fielding's fiction entitled, *Fielding and the Nature of the Novel* (1968).

WAYNE C. BOOTH (b. 1921) is Professor of English and Dean of the College at the University of Chicago. He is author of *The Rhetoric of Fiction* (1961).

R. S. CRANE (1886–1967) was Emeritus Distinguished Service Professor, University of Chicago, and one of the most respected and influential of modern critics. He edited *Modern Philology* (1930–52) and *Critics and Criticism Ancient and Modern* (1952) and was author of *The Languages of Criticism and the Structure of Poetry* (1953). His essays recently have been collected and published under the title *The Idea of the Humanities* (1967).

WILLIAM EMPSON (b. 1906), Professor of English Literature at Sheffield University, is one of the leading figures of modern criticism. His books include *Seven Types of Ambiguity* (1930), *Some Versions of Pastoral* (1935), *The Structure of Complex Words* (1951), *Milton's God* (1961), and two volumes of poetry (1935, 1940).

F. R. LEAVIS (b. 1895), Fellow of Downing College, Cambridge, was co-founder and editor of *Scrutiny: A Quarterly Review* (1932–53). One of the most controversial and provocative of contemporary critics, he has written numerous books, among them *Mass Civilization and Minority Culture* (1930), *D. H. Lawrence* (1930), *New Bearings in English Poetry* (1932), *Revaluation: Tradition and Development in English Poetry* (1936), *The Great Tradition* (1948), and *D. H. Lawrence: Novelist* (1955).

IAN WATT (b. 1917), Professor of English at Stanford University, is author of *The Rise of the Novel* (1957). His other publications include editions of Fielding's *Shamela* (1956) and Sterne's *Tristram Shandy* (1965) and the Twentieth Century Views volume on Jane Austen (1963).

ANDREW WRIGHT (b. 1923) is Professor of English at the University of California, San Diego. His books include *Jane Austen's Novels* (1953), *Joyce Cary* (1958), and *Henry Fielding: Mask and Feast* (1965).

Selected Bibliography

At present there is no satisfactory edition of *Tom Jones,* though many inexpensive reprints of the novel are available, the most useful of these being R. P. C. Mutter's paperback edition published by Penguin Books (1966). A reliable, fully annotated edition (text by Fredson Bowers, historical introduction and explanatory notes by M. C. Battestin) is in preparation, however, and will be published as part of the definitive Wesleyan Edition of Fielding's Works. One year after the publication of this scholarly, old-spelling edition of *Tom Jones,* M. C. Battestin will bring out in the Riverside series (Houghton Mifflin Company) a paperback edition of the novel with modernized text and with notes addressed to the general reader.

Despite its inaccuracies, the standard biography of Fielding is still Wilbur L. Cross's *The History of Henry Fielding* (New Haven, Conn.: Yale University Press, 1918), 3 vols., which also contains a full, though not always trustworthy, bibliography of Fielding's works. F. Homes Dudden's *Henry Fielding: His Life, Works, and Times* (Oxford: The Clarendon Press, 1952), 2 vols., adds nothing to Cross's research on the life and canon and repeats all his errors; however, Dudden's discussions of the novels and of the political and social background often are informative. On Fielding's ethical and religious views, see M. C. Battestin, *The Moral Basis of Fielding's Art* (Middletown, Conn.: Wesleyan University Press, 1959; 2nd printing, 1964) and Henry Knight Miller, *Essays on Fielding's 'Miscellanies': A Commentary on Volume One* (Princeton: Princeton University Press, 1961). The best brief introduction to Fielding and his writings is John Butt, *Fielding,* Writers and Their Work, No. 57 (London: Longmans, Green & Company, Ltd., 1954; revised 1959). A valuable collection of essays treating various aspects of Fielding's whole achievement as a writer is the companion volume to the present anthology: Ronald Paulson, ed., *Fielding: A Collection of Critical Essays,* Twentieth Century Views (Englewood Cliffs, N.J.: Prentice-Hall, Inc., 1962).

An excellent introduction to *Tom Jones,* containing perceptive discussions of Fielding's themes and techniques, is Irvin Ehrenpreis, *Fielding: Tom Jones,* Studies in English Literature, No. 23 (London: Edward Arnold, Publishers, 1964). Among the numerous other studies in print, the following books and articles approach the novel from a variety of viewpoints:

Alter, Robert. "The Picaroon Domesticated," in *Rogue's Progress: Studies in the Picaresque Novel.* Cambridge, Mass.: Harvard University Press, 1964. Argues that in *Tom Jones* the conventions of the picaresque novel are transformed and transcended, the form becoming an appropriate vehicle to express Fielding's Augustan faith in order and rationality.

Battestin, Martin C. "Osborne's *Tom Jones*: Adapting a Classic," *Virginia Quarterly Review*, XLII (1966), 378–93. On the film of the novel as a successful adaptation of Fielding's artistic techniques, if not of his meaning.

———. "Tom Jones and 'His *Egyptian* Majesty': Fielding's Parable of Government," *PMLA*, LXXXII (1967), 68–77. On the episode of gypsies as a satire against Jacobitism, with remarks on Fielding's use of allusion and metaphor.

Blanchard, Frederic T. *Fielding the Novelist: A Study in Historical Criticism.* New Haven, Conn.: Yale University Press, 1926. On the reception of Fielding's novels and their changing reputations.

Bliss, Michael. "Fielding's Bill of Fare in *Tom Jones*," *ELH*, XXX (1963), 236–43. On the function of the prefatory chapters in advancing the theme of "mutuality."

Coley, William B. "Gide and Fielding," *Comparative Literature*, XI (1959), 1–15. On Gide's interpretation of Fielding's morality and the function of the intrusive narrator in *Tom Jones*.

Digeon, Aurélien. *The Novels of Fielding.* London: Routledge & Kegan Paul, Ltd., 1925. This translation of Digeon's *Les Romans de Fielding* (Paris, 1923) includes a comprehensive discussion of characters and themes in *Tom Jones*; the best of the early critical essays on the novel.

Golden, Morris. *Fielding's Moral Psychology.* Amherst, Mass.: University of Massachusetts Press, 1966. On the tension in Fielding's moral system between self-love and social, between the philosophies of Locke and Mandeville on the one hand and of Shaftesbury and the Latitudinarians on the other.

Hatfield, Glenn W. "The Serpent and the Dove: Fielding's Irony and the Prudence Theme of *Tom Jones*," *Modern Philology*, LXV (1967), 17–32. Through irony Fielding in *Tom Jones* attempted to reclaim the "proper and original" moral sense of "prudence."

Hutchens, Eleanor N. *Irony in "Tom Jones."* University, Ala.: University of Alabama Press, 1965. On Fielding's use of the devices of "connotative irony," with particular reference to the theme of prudence in the novel.

Jensen, Gerard E. "Proposals for a Definitive Edition of Fielding's *Tom Jones*," *The Library*, XVIII (1937), 314–30. On Fielding's revisions of the novel.

Kettle, Arnold. *An Introduction to the English Novel*, Vol. I. London: Hutchinson University Library, 1951; New York: Harper Torchbooks, 1960. On Tom and Sophia as rebels against social convention and respectability as represented by Blifil. The discussion of *Tom Jones* is included in Paulson's anthology, cited in the headnote.

McKillop, Alan D. "Fielding," in *The Early Masters of English Fiction.* Lawrence: University of Kansas Press, 1956. A stimulating and scholarly discussion of Fielding's achievement as a novelist.

Miller, Henry K. "Some Functions of Rhetoric in *Tom Jones*," *Philological Quarterly*, XLV (1966), 209–35. On Fielding's use of the devices of classical rhetoric to enhance his comedy and to advance his moral themes.

Murry, John Middleton. "In Defence of Fielding," in *Unprofessional Essays.* London: Jonathan Cape Ltd., 1956. On Fielding's sexual ethic. The discussion of *Tom Jones* is included in Paulson.

Preston, John. "*Tom Jones* and the 'Pursuit of True Judgment,' " *ELH*, XXXIII (1966), 315–26. Argues that Fielding's theme is the necessity of forming accurate moral judgments.

Price, Martin. "Fielding: The Comedy of Forms," in *To the Palace of Wisdom: Studies in Order and Energy from Dryden to Blake*. New York: Doubleday & Company, Inc., 1964. Argues that the central theme in Fielding's work is the opposition between the generous feelings and the "forms" of self-justification.

Sacks, Sheldon. *Fiction and the Shape of Belief: A Study of Fielding with Glances at Swift, Johnson, and Richardson*. Berkeley and Los Angeles: University of California Press, 1964. An "Aristotelian" analysis, with emphasis on the example of Fielding, of the ways in which a novelist's moral beliefs are disclosed in his fiction.

Thornbury, Ethel Margaret. *Henry Fielding's Theory of the Comic Prose Epic*. University of Wisconsin Studies in Language and Literature, No. 30. Madison: University of Wisconsin Press, 1931. On the backgrounds of Fielding's theory of the novel as expressed in *Joseph Andrews* and *Tom Jones*. The catalogue of Fielding's library is reprinted in an appendix.

Van Ghent, Dorothy. "On *Tom Jones*," in *The English Novel: Form and Function*. New York: Holt, Rinehart & Winston, Inc., 1953; Harper Torchbooks, 1961. On the design of the novel and its relationship to the comic themes of "Nature" and "Fortune."